Bibliotherapy:
When Kids Need Books

✦

A Guide for Those in
Need of Reassurance

Amy Recob

iUniverse, Inc.
New York   Bloomington

Bibliotherapy: When Kids Need Books

A Guide for Those in Need of Reassurance

iUniverse books may be ordered through booksellers or by contacting:

iUniverse
1663 Liberty Drive
Bloomington, IN 47403
www.iuniverse.com
1-800-Authors (1-800-288-4677)

ISBN: 978-0-595-52530-0 (pbk)
ISBN: 978-0-595-62583-3 (ebk)

Printed in the United States of America

Dedication

To Jason, Gabriella, Drake, Tessa, and Kaliana for their support and love, and to my students whom I've learned so much from!

Introduction

Being a teacher has opened my eyes to the enormity of issues that our students and children are dealing with every day. <u>Bibliotherapy: When Kids Need Books</u> was written with the hope that by reading books about others dealing with similar issues and/or self-help books, these young people will be able to stop and recognize their issues, deal with them, and go on with life after some needed healing.

Bibliotherapy can also help those surrounding a young adult/child gain empathy. Empathy is defined as: "the intellectual identification with or vicarious experiencing of the feelings, thoughts, or attitudes of another" (dictionary.com). Bibliotherapy can be used by friends/family/teachers/ acquaintances of individuals dealing with problems that are difficult to understand. For example, a sibling of an individual who suffers from ADHD may gain a better understanding of why a brother/sister acts the way they do and thus, may be able to help the situation.

The books listed are intended for kids when they need some reassurance. Bibliotherapy is just that - book therapy. The books are suggestions, and by no means are an exhaustive list of every book out there. Feel free to write in your own books that you find along the way either under existing topics, or under the last section titled "Additional Books & Their Topics Found to Be Helpful"

For schools, it is recommended that efforts be made to have a variety of books available for children, including a sampling of books from each of the bibliotherapy topics addressed in this book.

The summaries* of books listed by issues are intended to match need, to interest and reading level.

---

*   Book summaries derived from the following sources: Amazon.com and BarnesandNoble.com summaries, including: Reed Business Information, Inc., School Library Journal, Publishers Weekly, Ingram, School Library Journal, Card catalog description, and Individual publisher's summaries

Contents

The Books By Topic

The Benefits of Bibliotherapy

Everyone has dealt with at least one of the issues listed in this book at some point in his/her lifetime. Whether that issue was conquered with the help of a loved one, through therapy, or is still weighing on the individual, the therapeutic power of a book is often overlooked. The reassurance gained when an individual learns that they are not the only one, can open several doors of communication, and can put one on the road to recovery or coming to terms with an issue.

In schools, bibliotherapy can greatly increase the connectivity of curriculum to the individual student. A genuine relation to a book can help students cope with their current situation. An added bonus is that with the increased interest, academic growth is more likely to occur.

In addition, those who want to help, but don't understand what their loved one is going through, can gain empathy by reading about a similar situation. This will better equip an individual to open the lines of communication with someone they care about.

HOW TO USE BIBLIOTHERAPY: THE PROCESS FOR THOSE IN NEED OF REASSURANCE:

1. The reader finds a book that addresses issues he/she is currently dealing with. That book should be appealing to the reader and at an appropriate reading level.
2. The reader sees that he/she is not alone when they identify with a character (usually the main character) in the book.
3. The reader becomes engrossed with the story as new realizations about the issues the reader is dealing with come to light.

4. The reader may become more comfortable/confident with his/her troubles.
5. With increased comfort and confidence, the reader may be more likely to open up to others and seek help/guidance. Or, solutions to one'sproblems may become evident without seeking out additional help.

How to Use Bibliotherapy: for Schools

1. Make this Bibliotherapy guide available to students.
   a. Pass the book around so everyone looks through it; those who really do need a specific issue addressed will not want to stand out from the crowd.
   b. Make a copy available in the school library so students can consult <u>Bibliotherapy: When Kids Need Books</u> on their own terms.
   c. As the teacher gets to know his/her students, the teacher can make book recommendations to students using this resource and their knowledge and concern of the students.
2. Give students a choice of what book they read for a class assignment (unfortunately, many young adults won't pick up a book on their own, without incentive).
3. Motivate students with introductory activities, such as exploring what the title might mean, what the student hopes to learn from the book, how the student can relate, etc.
4. Create an avenue for discussion during the book, such as:
   a. A reflective journal kept throughout the book
   b. Literature circle discussions where each student can discuss his/her book
   c. Letters to the main characters throughout
   d. Written alternatives to outcomes of the story
5. Closure is important. Concluding activities should include an in-depth reflection of the content of the book and how that may or may not have related to the student. Students should be able to rate the book and state what they might have done as the author to make the book better.

How To Use Bibliotherapy: for Parents

1. Either use this guide to make a recommendation for your child, or make this book available for your child to choose his/her own book.
2. Help your child get the desired book.
3. Ask questions about the book.

2. Make yourself available to discuss any questions/revelations as your child reads.

How to Use Bibliotherapy: for Those Who Seek Understanding of a Loved One

1. Find a desirable book under the topic your loved one is dealing with.
2. As you read, discover connections between the book and your loved one.
3. If you and your loved one are comfortable with it, ask questions about discoveries made during your reading.

Abandonment

Anderson, Susan. <u>The Journey from Abandonment to Healing</u>. Berkley Publishing Group, 2000. (Grades 9 and up)
  ~ Anderson's book defines the five phases of a different kind of grieving—grieving over a lost relationship. *The Journey from Abandonment to Healing* is designed to help all victims of emotional breakups--whether they are suffering from a recent loss, or a lingering wound from the past; whether they are caught up in patterns that sabotage their own relationships, or they're in a relationship where they no longer feel loved.

Ballard, Kimberly M. <u>Light at Summer's End</u>. WaterBrook Press, 1994. (Grades 8 and up)
  ~ Dumped off at a lady's house for the summer, fourteen-year-old Melissa and her new guardian develop a friendship as they work through the hurts of the past and grapple with the issue of abortion.

Bassham, Lizann. <u>Barefoot</u>. Booksurge Publishing, 2006. (Grades 7 and up)
  ~ After Opal's mother is killed in an accident, she is sent to live with her grandmother and begins to learn of her family's history of abandonment.

Black, Claudia. <u>It Will Never Happen to Me</u>. Ballantine Books, 1991. (Grades 8 and up)
  ~ Claudia Black offers help to the most neglected members of the alcoholic family--the 28 million children of alcoholics in America today. She shows how to understand roles, deal with problems, and break destructive patterns of behavior.

Buckman, Michelle. <u>Maggie Come Lately</u>. NavPublishing Group, 2007.
　　　(Grades 7 and up)
　　　～ At age 4, Maggie witnessed her mother's suicide. Since then, Maggie
　　　has been the parent, housekeeper, and the responsible person in the
　　　house since her dad has abandoned his responsibilities, including her
　　　two younger brothers. At age 16, Maggie has found a new identity as
　　　a popular person, and is struggling with who she really is and what
　　　her values are. She really comes into her own after a sexual assault.

Byng, Georgia. <u>Molly Moon's Incredible Book of Hypnotism</u>. Harper
　　　Collins, 2003. (Grades 5-9)
　　　～The book is about lonely, unwanted orphan Molly Moon who lives
　　　at Hardwick house, a terrible orphanage. When Molly discovers a
　　　book on hypnotism she discovers that this is a talent that she is good
　　　at. She uses her new found powers to her advantage.

Creech, Sharon. <u>Ruby Holler</u>. HarperTrophy, 2004. (Grades 5-8)
　　　～ Dallas and Florida are orphans who appear hopeless and rebellious.
　　　Tiller and Sairy are an older couple who invite the twins to join
　　　them on their journeys. Through the magic of Ruby Holler they all
　　　grow closer and grow up.

Cushway, Karen. <u>Rodzina</u>. Scholastic Press, 2004. (Grades 6-10)
　　　～ Set in 1881, this is a story of a young girl traveling by train. Her
　　　destination is either a loving home, or a life of a servant.

Desetta, Al, M.A. and Wolin, Sybil, Ph.D. <u>The Struggle to Be Strong True</u>
　　　<u>Stories by Teens About Overcoming Tough Times.</u> Free Spirit
　　　Publishing. (Grades 7 and up)
　　　～ In 30 first-person accounts, teens tell how they overcame major
　　　life obstacles, including, drug abuse by loved ones, interracial
　　　relationships, abandonment, homosexuality, and more.

Frost, Helen. <u>Keesha's House</u>. Farrar, Straus, and Giroux, 2003. (Grades
　　　9 and up)
　　　～ Joe's mother died when he was young. His aunt took him in when
　　　he was 12, and he now owns that house. Keesha's dad is a mean
　　　drunk so Joe takes her in. Also in the book is a pregnant 16 year old,
　　　a young man whose father threw him because he is gay, a victim of
　　　sexual abuse, a child who's been abandoned then ends up in juvie, a
　　　child whose parents are in jail

Fusco, Kimberly Newton. <u>Tending to Grace</u>. Laurel-Leaf Books, 2005.
　　　(Grades 7-12)

~ When Cornelia is abandoned by her mother, she has to fend for herself. Because of her profound stutter, she keeps quiet and stays in remedial classes, despite her desire to be in honors English. She eventually finds someone like her to confide in.

Gantos, Jack. <u>Joey Pigza Loses Control</u>. HarperTrophy, 2002. (Grades 6-9)
~ Now that Joey has a handle on his actions, he feels prepared to face his estranged father, Carter Pigza. The only problem is that Joey's dad is just as wired as Joey used to be. When Carter flushes his meds, Joey has to decide if being friends with his dad is worth losing his hard-won self-control.

Gregory, Kristiana. <u>Orphan Runaways</u>. Scholastic, 1998. (Grades 5-10)
~ *Orphan Runaways* is about two orphan brothers, 12 year old Danny and 6 year old Judd, who search for their uncle in the California gold camps after their parents die in an epidemic.

Hambrook, Diane. <u>A Mother Loss Workbook : Healing Exercises for Daughters</u>. Perennial, 1997. (Grades 6 and up)
~ *A Mother Loss Workbook* is designed to help the motherless daughter tell the story she needs to tell--her story. Its varied exercises provide both careful direction and room for self-expression. This book is a safe place where no one will judge a woman, where the work she must do can be done in her own time, at her own pace, and at any stage of mourning.

Holz, Loretta. <u>Foster Child</u>. Messner, 1981. (Grades 5-8)
~ After Peter's dad leaves and his mother begins drinking heavily, he is placed in foster care.

Inclan, Jessica Barksdale. <u>Her Daughter's Eyes</u>. New American Library, 2001. (Grades 9 and up)
~ Kate Phillips--17 years old, unmarried, and pregnant--and her younger sister Tyler have been abandoned by their parents. Cancer took their beloved mother two years before, and their father has emotionally left them, choosing to spend his time with his new girlfriend. Kate insists that her baby's existence must remain hidden, but inevitably, the sisters' secrets are discovered, involving the police and children's protective services.

Karl, Jean. <u>Beloved Benjamin is Waiting</u>. Dutton, 1978. (Grades 4 and up)
~ After her mother's disappearance, Lucinda takes refuge in a caretaker's shack in the local cemetary

Martin, Ann M. <u>Here Today</u>. Scholastic Press, 2004. (Grades 5-8)

- Ellie's mom, "Doris," is most often away from home trying to become famous, and her Dad works very long hours. As if that weren't bad enough, Ellie's mom eventually actually runs away to New York and ends up working in a department store instead of being discovered.

Simon, Norma. I Wish I Had My Father. Albert Whitman, 1987. (Grades 2-6)
- Father's Day is tough for a boy whose father left him years ago and never communicates with him.

Stewart, Bridgett, and White, Franklin. No Matter What. Blue/Black Press, 2002. (Grades 7-12)
- Bridgett Stewart shares her journey through unthinkable poverty and discusses everything from gaining her own self-respect when no one else would respect her because of where she lived to surviving verbal abuse from classmates, living without a father, school pressures, and her decision to use education as a vehicle from poverty while earning a 4.0 grade point average in tough and trying times. Stewart also discusses self-esteem, alcohol and drugs, and many other topics.

Voigt, Cynthia. Homecoming. Simon Pulse, 2002. (Grades 6 and up)
- Dicey and her younger siblings, abandoned by their mother in a shopping mall, make their way to Virginia and their grandmother.

Voigt, Cynthia. Solitary Blue. Aladdin Library, 2003. (Grades 7-12)
- Jeff Greene was only seven when Melody, his mother, left him with his reserved, undemonstrative father, the Professor. Years later, she comes back and has Jeff spend the summer with her. During his second summer with her, he is betrayed.

Woodson, Jacqueline. I Hadn't Meant to Tell You This. Laurel-Leaf, 1995. (Grades 7 and up)
- Two girls: one white, one black; one abused, one protected, both missing their mothers. An unlikely friendship ignites between the two, and, in sharing their differences, both of their lives are transformed.

Abortion

Baker, Keri. <u>Once in a Green Room</u>. Science & Humanities Press, 2001. (Grades 10 and up)
    ~ After being raped and having an abortion while in college, a young woman struggles to deal with her feelings and is ultimately helped by the insights she gains from her special education students.

Ballard, Kimberly M. <u>Light at Summer's End</u>. WaterBrook Press, 1994. (Grades 8 and up)
    ~ Dumped off at a lady's house for the summer, fourteen-year-old Melissa and her new guardian develop a friendship as they work through the hurts of the past and grapple with the issue of abortion.

Beckman, Gunnel. <u>Mia Alone</u>. Random House Children's Books, 1978. (Grades 7 and up)
    ~ A young Swedish girl deliberates the pros and cons of having an abortion and finds it is a decision she must make alone.

Heckert, Connie K. <u>To Keera with Love: Abortion, Adoption, or Keeping the Baby, the Story of One Teen's Choice</u>. Rowman & Littlefield Publishers, Inc., 1989. (Grades 8 and up)
    ~ Takes the reader through the decision process once a pregnancy is discovered

Nykiel, Connie. <u>No One Told Me I Could Cry: A Teen's Guide to Hope and Healing after Abortion</u>. Life Cycle Books, 1997. (Grades 9 and up)
    ~ The aftermath of an abortion is discussed.

Ponton, Lynn, MD. <u>The Sex Lives of Teenagers: Revealing the Secret</u>
<u>World of Adolescent Boys and Girls</u>. Plume Books, 2001.
(Grades 9 and up)
~ With more and more teenagers having sex by the age of sixteen and
others feeling pressured to before they're ready, parents and adolescents
must find ways to communicate openly and honestly about a subject
that has been ignored for too long. Lynn Ponton, M.D., takes a look
at what teenagers have to say about their sexual lives. In a safe forum,
without fear of judgment or censorship, teens feel free to speak frankly
about their feelings, desires, fantasies, and expectations. And parents
give voice to the struggle of coming to terms with their children's
emerging sexual identities. Dr. Ponton opens a dialogue that addresses
controversial topics such as pregnancy, abortion, masturbation, sexual
orientation, Internet dating, and gender roles. Sensitive subjects such
as AIDS and drugs are also explored.

Saul, Laya. <u>You Don't Have to Learn Everything the Hard Way: What</u>
<u>I Wish Someone Had Told Me</u>. Kadima Press, 2004. (Grades
8 and up)
~ Reading this book first can help young adults avoid dangerous
situations and possible regrets later on. Ms. Saul shares her life
lessons with young adults, including the following topics: Defining
Boundaries, Gaining a New Perspective, Expecting the Unexpected,
Choices that Change Your Life, Dealing with Failure and Regret, Pain
and Suffering as Part of Living, Alcohol and Drug Abuse, Preventing
Abuse, Life and Death, You and the World, Relationships, Family
and Friends, Forgiveness, and Live Your Dreams.

Swisher, Karin L., Leone, Bruno, and O'Neil, Terry. <u>Teenage Sexuality:</u>
<u>Opposing Viewpoints</u>. Gale Group, 1994. (Grades 9 and up)
~ An examination of birth control, sex education, STDs,
homosexuality, pregnancy, and changes in the attitudes toward
teenage sexuality and morality. The book explores a wide range of
opinions and perspectives. *(Doris A. Fong)*

Zimmerman, Martha. <u>Should I Keep My Baby?</u> Bethany House Publishers,
1983. (Grades 8 and up)
~ The author offers straight-to-the-heart advice on getting immediate
medical attention, knowing who to tell, evaluating your alternatives,
choosing life for your baby rather than aborting, deciding if you're
ready for marriage and motherhood, understanding adoption.

Adoption

Bawden, Nina. <u>The Finding</u>. Lothrop, 1985. (Grades 5-8)
    ~ Alex runs away from his adoptive family during a crisis, but returns at the end of the crisis.

Bishop, Sheila. <u>A Speaking Likeness</u>. Hurst and Blackett, 1976. (Grades 9-12)
    ~ Diana, a widowed mom, meets a young pregnant woman who is sick. After birth, the young woman wants nothing to do with the baby. Diana plans to adopt the baby, but discovers who the child's father is while on holiday.

Burgess, Linda Cannon. <u>The Art of Adoption</u>. Norton, 1981. (Grades 10-adult)
    ~ This book was written for the adoptee, birth parents, adoptive parents, and prospective adoptive parents. The technicalities are addressed.

Cohen, Shari. <u>Coping With Being Adopted</u>. Rosen, 1988. (Grades 6-12)
    ~ The common problems of adoption are addressed, including transracial and handicapped adoptees.

Girard, Linda. <u>We Adopted You, Benjamin Koo</u>. Whitman, 1989. (Grades 1-4)
    ~ Benjamin Koo Andrews, of Korean descent, tells what it's like to be adopted into an American family.

Johnson, Angela. The First Part of Last. Simon & Schuster Children's Publishing, 2003. (Grades 8 and up)
~ Bobby is your classic urban teenaged boy -- impulsive, eager, restless. On his sixteenth birthday his girlfriend, Nia tells him she's pregnant. Bobby's going to be a father. Suddenly things like school and house parties and hanging with friends no longer seem important as they're replaced by visits to Nia's obstetrician and a social worker who says that the only way for Nia and Bobby to lead a normal life is to put their baby up for adoption. Johnson looks at the male side of teen pregnancy as she delves into one young man's struggle to figure out what "the right thing" is and then to do it. No matter what the cost.

Krementz, Jill. How it Feels to Be Adopted. Knopf, 1988. (Grades 9 & up)
~ Interviews with adopted children and adoptive families about their experiences and feelings concerning adoption.

Lapsley, Susan. I Am Adopted. Random House of Canada, 1987. (Grades K-3)
~ A young boy explains what it means to be adopted.

Lifton, Betty Jean. I'm Still Me. Knopf Books for Young Readers, 1981. (Grades 9 & up)
~ A history assignment to explore her roots motivates a high school junior into a search for her biological parents.

Lowry, Lois. Find a Stranger Say Goodbye. Laurel Leaf, 1990. (Grades 7-12)
~ The story of a teenager who is looking for her birth parents

Nerlove, Evelyn. Who is David? Child Welfare League of America, 1985. (Grades 7-9)
~ A story of an adopted adolescent and his friends. This book gives the adoptee and his parents insight into the confusion felt by adopted adolescents.

Neufeld, John. Edgar Allan. Puffin, 1999. (Grades 4-8)
~ A family adopts a young boy who is of a different race in the 1950's.

Noonan, Michael. December Boys. University of Queensland Press, 1990. (Grades 9-12)
~ Five orphans are spending their Christmas with a family. There is competition as one of the orphans will be adopted.

Orcutt, Jane. Lullaby. Tyndale House Publishers, 2002. (Grades 9 and up)

~ Merrilee wants only the best for the child she cannot keep. Nora dreams of being a mother to a child of her own. Lullaby is a Christian story of a courageous teenage girl and a woman who longs for a baby.

Paterson, Katherine.   <u>Great Gilly Hopkins</u>.   Harper Trophy, 2004. (Grades 5-9)
~ A "tough" girl learns what it's like to be accepted and loved by a family.

Powledge, Fred. <u>So You're Adopted</u>. Atheneum, 1982. (Grades 7 & up)
~ Examines the personal concerns and questions that sometimes rouble adopted youngsters and their families.

Williamson, Kristin. <u>Princess Kate</u>. (Grades 6-10)
~ The story of a 14 year old, who discovers she is adopted, and her need to find her birthmother.

Aids

Arrick, Fran. <u>What You Don't Know Can Kill You</u>. Delacorte Books for
Young Readers, 1992. (Grades 9-12)
- Ellen, college-bound in the fall, learns that she carries the HIV
virus, transmitted to her by her previously monogamous, slightly
older boyfriend, who had engaged in unsafe sex after getting drunk
at a fraternity house.

Bell, Ruth. <u>Changing Bodies, Changing Lives: A Book for Teens on Sex and
Relationships.</u> Vintage Books USA, 1988. (Grades 8 and up)
- Addresses the need for open dialogue between teenagers on
the topics of sex and relationships. Informs them on how to
prevent unwanted pregnancies and sexually transmitted diseases.
Updated to include material on suicide, AIDS and food and
drug abuse.

Curran, Christine Perdan. <u>Sexually Transmitted Diseases</u>. Enslow Publishers,
Incorporated, 1998. (Grades 8 and up)
- Examines the history, symptoms, treatment, and prevention of
such sexually transmitted diseases as syphilis, gonorrhea, herpes,
AIDS, and hepatitis.

Gleitzman, Morris. <u>Two Weeks With Queen</u>. HarperTrophy, 1993.
(Grades 7-12)
- Colin, who was once self-centered, matures rapidly as his brother is
diagnosed with cancer and he finds an unlikely friend whose partner
is dying from AIDS.

Gravelle, Karen, et al. <u>What's Going on Down There: Answers to Questions Boys Find Hard to Ask</u>. Walker & Company, 1998. (Grades 9 and up)
~ Describes the physical and emotional changes that occur in boys (and, to a lesser extent, in girls) during puberty and discusses sexual activity, homosexuality, AIDS, and other related topics.

Miklowitz, Gloria. <u>Goodbye Tomorrow</u>. Delacorte Books for Young Readers, 1987. (Grades 9-12)
~ A popular teen athlete learns he has AIDS from a blood transfusion after his car accident.

Palardy, Debra J. <u>Sweetie Here's the Best Reason on the Planet to Say No to Your Boyfriend: Even If You've Already Said Yes</u>. Dorrance Pub Co, 2000. (Grades 8 and up)
~ This book is for adolescents who may have felt pressured to engage in activities in which they were not always comfortable or completely willing. It addresses the issue of changing morals in schools and concerns that this may be enough to make even the most straight-laced young lady feel that sexual activity is okay. Author Debra J. Palardy presents a collection of lines used by hormone-driven teenage boys to get their girlfriends to engage in sex. She follows through and provides useful comeback and advice for girls, considering their boyfriends' pleas. The author provides the objective wisdom sought by teenagers too embarrassed, timid, or afraid to consult those closet to them. Her guide points out the pitfalls of becoming sexually active, including pregnancy, sexually transmitted disease, and loss of self-esteem. She urges teenage girls to seek guidance from women who have had the time to develop an adult perspective and look back on their own experiences.

Ponton, Lynn, MD. <u>The Sex Lives of Teenagers: Revealing the Secret World of Adolescent Boys and Girls</u>. Plume Books, 2001. (Grades 9 and up)
~ With more and more teenagers having sex by the age of sixteen and others feeling pressured to before they're ready, parents and adolescents must find ways to communicate openly and honestly about a subject that has been ignored for too long. Lynn Ponton, M.D., takes a look at what teenagers have to say about their sexual lives. In a safe forum, without fear of judgment or censorship, teens feel free to speak frankly about their feelings, desires, fantasies, and expectations. And parents give voice to the struggle of coming to terms with their children's emerging sexual identities. Dr.

Ponton opens a dialogue that addresses controversial topics such as pregnancy, abortion, masturbation, sexual orientation, Internet dating, and gender roles. Sensitive subjects such as AIDS and drugs are also explored.

Sparks, Beatrice. <u>It Happened to Nancy</u>. Avon, 1994. (Grades 9 & up)
    - A teenaged victim of AIDS recounts her battle with the disease in her diary, describing her first love, the night she was date-raped, her diagnosis of AIDS, and her thoughts and dreams.

Aging Grandparents

DePaola, Tomie. <u>Now One Foot, Now the Other</u>. Putnam, 1981. (Grade K-4)
    - When his grandfather Bob suffers a stroke, Bobby teaches him to walk again, just as his grandfather had once taught him.

Dugin, Barbara. <u>Loop-the-Loop</u>. Greenwillow, 1992. (Grades 4-8)
    - A young girl and an old woman form a friendship that lasts even after the woman enters a nursing home.

Johnston, Tony. <u>Grandpa's Song</u>. Dial, 1991. (Grades K-4)
    - When a young girl's beloved grandfather becomes forgetful, she helps him remember the words to his favorite song.

Zindel, Paul. <u>The Pigman</u>. Starfire, 1983. (Grades 8 and up)
    ~ Loraine and John learn a lot about themselves from the once victim of their phone prank, the Pigman. Up to this point, they've struggled to find any meaning in their lives.

Alcohol Abuse

Black, Claudia. It Will Never Happen to Me. Ballantine Books, 1991.
(Grades 8 and up)
  ~ Claudia Black offers help to the most neglected members of the
alcoholic family--the 28 million children of alcoholics in America
today. She shows how to understand roles, deal with problems, and
break destructive patterns of behavior.

Bo, Ben. Skullcrack. Lernersports, 2000. (Grades 4-8)
  ~ Jonah does his best to deal with his alcoholic father and makes
some bad choices along the way. He learns to surf and also finds out
he has a twin.

Draper, Sharon. Tears of a Tiger. Simon Pulse, 1996. (Grades 6-12)
  ~ A high school basketball star struggles with guilt and depression
following the drunk-driving accident that killed his best friend.
Short chapters and alternating view points provide "raw energy and
intense emotion," said Publishers Weekly.

Friend, Natasha. Lush. Scholastic Paperbacks, 2006. (Grades 6-12)
  ~ The main character, Samantha, is dealing with her father's alcoholism
and her mother's denial of the problem. Because Samantha has a
younger brother, she feels that she needs to protect him. She begins
a correspondence to seek help.

Frost, Helen. Keesha's House. Farrar, Straus, and Giroux, 2003. (Grades
9 and up)
  ~ Joe's mother died when he was young. His aunt took him in when
he was 12, and he now owns that house. Keesha's dad is a mean

drunk so Joe takes her in. Also in the book is a pregnant 16 year old, a young man whose father threw him out because he is gay, a victim of sexual abuse, a child who's been abandoned then ends up in juvie, a child whose parents are in jail

le, Erica. Catch the Sun. Rainbow Publishing, 1987. (Grades 9-12)
~ Fed up with her drunken stepfather and her dead end job Lennie runs away.

Holz, Loretta. Foster Child. Messner, 1981. (Grades 5-8)
~ After Peter's dad leaves and his mother begins drinking heavily, he is placed in foster care.

Mazer, Harry. The War on Villa Street. Delacort, 1978. (Grades 5-9)
~ Willis, an eight year old, is frequently beaten by his alcoholic father. After striking back at his father, Willis runs away but returns, hoping things will improve.

McCoy, Kathy, and Wibbelsman, Charles, M.D. Life Happens: A Teenager's Guide to Friends, Failure, Sexuality, Love, Rejection, Addiction, Peer Pressure, Families, Loss, Depression, Change, and Other challenges. Berkley Publishing, 1996. Grades 7-12)
~ Offers advice on how to cope with such feelings as sadness, anger, and anxiety related to various problems including the death of a family member, teen pregnancy, the end of a romantic relationship, being homosexual, and having an alcoholic parent.

Packer, Alex J., Ph.D. HIGHS! Over 150 Ways to Feel Really, REALLY Good…Without Alcohol or Other Drugs. Free Spirit Publishing. (Grades 7 and up)
~ Packer outlines natural highs, such as: breathing and meditation, sports and exercise, food, the senses, nature, creativity, family, friends, and more.

Paulsen, Gary. Alida's Song. Yearling, 2001. (Grades 5-8)
~ A 14-year-old boy overcomes his parents' alcoholism and his own destructive and negative path when his grandmother invites him to work for the summer.

Quarles, Heather. A Door Near Here. Laurel Leaf, 2000. (Grades 8 and up)
~ Fifteen year old Katharine has to mature too soon to try to conceal the fact that her mother is an alcoholic. She is trying to keep the family together.

Rebman, Renee. <u>Addictions and Risky Behaviors: Cutting, Bingeing, Snorting, and Other Risky Behaviors</u>. Enslow Publishers, Incorporated, 2006.

    ~The causes and signs of these addictions are addressed by Rebman. Also addressed is how those who are addicted can be helped.

Saul, Laya. <u>You Don't Have to Learn Everything the Hard Way: What I Wish Someone Had Told Me</u>. Kadima Press, 2004. (Grades 8 and up)

    ~ Reading this book first can help young adults avoid dangerous situations and possible regrets later on. Ms. Saul shares her life lessons with young adults, including the following topics: Defining Boundaries, Gaining a New Perspective, Expecting the Unexpected, Choices that Change Your Life, Dealing with Failure and Regret, Pain and Suffering as Part of Living, Alcohol and Drug Abuse, Preventing Abuse, Life and Death, You and the World, Relationships, Family and Friends, Forgiveness, and Live Your Dreams.

Stewart, Bridgett, and White, Franklin. <u>No Matter What</u>. Blue/Black Press, 2002. (Grades 7-12)

    ~ Bridgett Stewart shares her journey through unthinkable poverty and discusses everything from gaining her own self-respect when no one else would respect her because of where she lived to surviving verbal abuse from classmates, living without a father, school pressures, and her decision to use education as a vehicle from poverty while earning a 4.0 grade point average in tough and trying times.

    Stewart also discusses self-esteem, alcohol and drugs, and many other topics.

Stewart, Maureen. <u>Vicki's Habit</u>. Penguin Books Ltd, 1987. (Grades 9-12)

    ~ Vicki and her friends have been drinking together since they were eleven. Now they are fifteen and their drinking is getting more and more serious. Vicki writes about her feelings, her life, her alcohol consumption and many other topics

Wagner, Robin S. and Wagner, Robert. <u>Sarah T.: The Portrait of a Teenage Alcoholic</u>. Random House, Incorporated, 1975. (Grades 9 and up)

    ~ Teen-age problem drinkers are not just young adults of legal age. Many are alcoholics at 12 and 13, and some even sooner. *Sarah T.— Portrait Of A Teen- Age Alcoholic* takes both a shocking and compassionate look at the growing problem of adolescent liquor abuse ... and the desperate need for rehabilitation.

Anger

Cohen-Sandler, Roni and Silver, Michelle. I'm Not Mad, I Just Hate You!: A New Understanding of Mother-Daughter Conflict. Penguin, 2000. (Grades 9 and up)
- Teen girls, who are socialized to stifle their anger and avoid confrontation, frequently take out their frustration on their mothers as the only safe and available targets. *I'm Not Mad, I Just Hate You!* combines the expertise of a clinical psychologist (who has worked with women and adolescent girls for more than twenty years) with that of a senior editor at a leading teen magazine. The book demonstrates how mother-daughter friction during adolescence, managed creatively, empowers girls by teaching them invaluable skills and can even foster intimacy.

Cullen, Murray and Wright, Joan. Cage Your Rage for Teens: A Guide to Anger Control. American Correctional Association, 1996. (Grades 8 and up)
- A source of help for adolescents who struggle with anger management

Bolme, Sarah. Keep Your Cool! Control Your Anger Before It Controls You! Oakwood Publishing, 2002. (Grades 7 and up)
- Bolme uses real-life situations that relate to teens and will likely increase their willingness to engage in her interactive book and learn about and manage their anger.

Egeberg, Gary. My Feelings Are Like Wild Animals: How Do I Tame Them? : A Practical Guide to Help Teens (And Former Teens) Feel and Deal With Painful Emotions. Paulist Press, 1998. (Grades 7 and up)

~ Uses a Christian perspective to explain how to deal with difficult, unpleasant, or painful emotions such as anger, anxiety, hate, and fear.

Flinn, Alex. <u>Breathing Underwater</u>. HarperTempest, 2002. (Grade 9 and up)
~ In this book, a girl named Cat is abused by her jealous boyfriend. Nick is only jealous because he loves Caitlin with all his heart. Partially because Nick was abused by his father, he doesn't know how else he should express his feelings. He truly loves Cat, but is also truly hurting her.

Gaynor, Darlyne, Ph.D., Nemeth, Kelly Paulk, Ph.D, Schexnayder, and Maydel Morin. <u>Helping Your Angry Child: Worksheets, Fun Puzzles, and Engaging Games to Help You Communicate Better : A Workbook for You and Your Family.</u> New Harbinger Publications, 2003. (Grades 6 and up)
~ Consumer text offers interactive, real-world solutions for helping a child deal with anger and rage. Teaches essential skills to help the parent cope with a child's anger by applying anger-management skills, listening skills, and labeling the child's anger. Includes exercises and games for the child, diet and relaxation tips.

Kellner, Millicent. <u>In Control: A Skill-Building Program for Teaching Young Adolescents to Manage Anger</u>. Research Press (IL), 2001. (Grades 9 and up)
~ A guide to helping youth overcome their anger

McCoy, Kathy, and Wibbelsman, Charles, M.D. <u>Life Happens: A Teenager's Guide to Friends, Failure, Sexuality, Love, Rejection, Addiction, Peer Pressure, Families, Loss, Depression, Change, and Other challenges.</u> Berkley Publishing, 1996. (Grades 7-12)
~ Offers advice on how to cope with such feelings as sadness, anger, and anxiety related to various problems including the death of a family member, teen pregnancy, the end of a romantic relationship, being homosexual, and having an alcoholic parent

Peterson, Jean Sunde. <u>Talk with Teens about Feelings, Family, Relationships and the Future, Grades 7-12: 50 Guided Discussions for School and Counseling Groups</u>. Free Spirit Publishing, Inc., 1997. (Grades 7-12)
~ Fifty guided discussions on mood swings, anger, sadness, sexual behavior, violence, dating, career choices, and more help students share their feelings and concerns and know they are not alone.

Saul, Laya. <u>You Don't Have to Learn Everything the Hard Way: What I Wish Someone Had Told Me</u>. Kadima Press, 2004. (Grades 8 and up)

~ Reading this book first can help young adults avoid dangerous situations and possible regrets later on. Ms. Saul shares her life lessons with young adults, including the following topics: Defining Boundaries, Gaining a New Perspective, Expecting the Unexpected, Choices that Change Your Life, Dealing with Failure and Regret, Pain and Suffering as Part of Living, Alcohol and Drug Abuse, Preventing Abuse, Life and Death, You and the World, Relationships, Family and Friends, Forgiveness, and Live Your Dreams.

Seaward, Brian. <u>Hot Stones and Funny Bones : Teens Helping Teens Cope with Stress and Anger</u>. Health Communications, 2002. (Grades 7-12)

~ Provides an inside look at ways in which teens cope with their stress and anger, such as keeping a journal, meditating, or having a good laugh, and includes advice for parents and other teens.

Simmons, Rachel. <u>Odd Girl Out: The Hidden Culture of Aggression in Girls</u>. Harcourt Brace & Company, 2003. (Grades 9 and up)

~ Why are girls becoming more aggressive in their everyday lives, and how is it affecting their overall self-esteem? Rachel Simmons, a Rhodes scholar who has painstakingly researched female bullying and the psychology of girls, feels that girls' aggressiveness is just as harmful as that of boys but is much harder to recognize.

Thompson, Tate. <u>Senioritis</u>. May Davenport, 2003. (Grades 9 and up)

~ A group of high school teenagers have to attend a 3-5 p.m. program to make up credits, or to correct inappropriate behavior before they can graduate. A very compassionate mentor encourages them to correct their failings as they vent their anger against teachers in their journals. The biggest strength of this novel is that low or high level readers can pick up this book and find at least one character who they know, or who they actually are.

Weill, Sabrina Solin. <u>We're Not Monsters: Teens Speak Out about Teens in Trouble</u>. HarperTempest, 2002. (Grades 8 – 12)

~ Each chapter offers a variety of the issues including school shootings, anxiety, suicide, self-injury, and sex crimes, facts and statistics, plus advice and the voices of teenagers themselves. Weill also includes suggestions for further reading as well as phone numbers and Web addresses of organizations designed to help.

Wilde, Jerry. Hot Stuff to Help Kids Chill Out: The Anger Management
      Book. Lgr. Publishing, 1997. (Grades 5-10)
      - This book designed to encourage today's youth to manage their
      anger rather than be controlled by it.

Wilde, Jerry. More Hot Stuff to Help Kids Chill Out: The Anger and Stress
      Management Book. Lgr Productions, 2001. (Grades 5-10)
      - This book contains many helpful activities that demonstrate to
      kids that they have the ability to change their thoughts and change
      their feelings.

Anxiety/stress

Abeel, Samantha. <u>My Thirteenth Winter: A Memoir</u>. Scholastic, Inc., 2003.
(Grades 6-12)
~ Samantha Abeel tells her own story of living with and overcoming dyscalculia. She describes in painstaking detail how her life was affected by her learning disability before and after she was diagnosed, and the way her peers, her family, and her teachers treated her. In seventh grade, Samantha suffered anxiety attacks as she struggled to keep up in her classes, to remember two locker combinations, and to deal with new teachers. Samantha was eventually placed in Special Education classes in eighth grade, but she continued to feel anxious about her future.

Bayer, Linda N. <u>Uneasy Lives: Understanding Anxiety Disorder</u>. Chelsea House Publishers, 2000. (Grades 7 and up)
~ Examines various anxiety disorders, including panic attacks, phobias, agoraphobia, obsessive-compulsive disorder, and post-traumatic stress.

Egeberg, Gary. <u>My Feelings Are Like Wild Animals: How Do I Tame Them? : A Practical Guide to Help Teens (And Former Teens) Feel and Deal With Painful Emotions</u>. Paulist Press, 1998. (Grades 7 and up)
~ Uses a Christian perspective to explain how to deal with difficult, unpleasant, or painful emotions such as anger, anxiety, hate, and fear.

Elkind, David. All Grown Up and No Place to Go: Teenagers in Crisis. Perseus Books Group, 1997. (Grades 9 and up)
- Elkind makes a case for protecting teens instead of pressuring them. This book addresses long work hours, rising violence, and pregnancies.

Fox, Annie, M.Ed. and Kirschner, Ruth. Too Stressed to Think? A Teen Guide to Staying Sane When Life Makes You Crazy. Free Spirit Publishing. (Grades 7 and up)
- This book includes practical information and stress-lessening tools teens can use every day. Realistic scenarios describe stressful situations teen readers can relate to.

Hipp, Earl and Fleishman, Michael. Fighting Invisible Tigers: A Stress Management Guide for Teens (Teen-Focused Coping Skills). Free Spirit Publishing, 1995. (Grades 6-12)
- Discusses the pressures and problems encountered by teenagers and provides information on life skills, stress management, and methods of gaining more control over their lives.

Huebner, Dawn. What to do When You Worry Too Much: a Kid's Guide to Overcoming Anxiety. Magination Press, 2005. (Grades 5-8)
- Guides kids through how to help themselves to overcome their anxiety. Gives motivation and guidance.

Luciani, Joseph. Self-Coaching: How to Heal Anxiety and Depression. Wiley, 2001. Grades 9 and up
- Self-Coaching will show you how to: develop a fresh way of thinking, leading to a healthy, adaptive way of living, follow winning strategies so you can accomplish what you want in life, use the self-talk technique to coach yourself back to health.

McCoy, Kathy, and Wibbelsman, Charles, M.D. Life Happens: A Teenager's Guide to Friends, Failure, Sexuality, Love, Rejection, Addiction, Peer Pressure, Families, Loss, Depression, Change, and Other challenges. Berkley Publishing, 1996. (Grades 7-12)
- Offers advice on how to cope with such feelings as sadness, anger, and anxiety related to various problems including the death of a family member, teen pregnancy, the end of a romantic relationship, being homosexual, and having an alcoholic parent

Powell, Mark, and Adams, Kelly. Stress Relief: The Ultimate Teen Guide (It Happened to Me, 3). Scarecrow Press, 2003. (Grades 6-12)

⁓ Describes the causes of stress, how to recognize and deal with them, and how to alleviate the stress itself by using such methods as breathing exercises, meditation, and creative visualization.

Roehlkepartain, Jolene. <u>Surviving School Stress</u>. Group Pub Inc., 1990. (Grades 6-12)

    ⁓ Focuses on school-related stress and how to deal with it from a Christian perspective. Discusses grades, parents' expectations, after-school activities, and getting along with people who have different beliefs.

Saul, Laya. <u>You Don't Have to Learn Everything the Hard Way: What I Wish Someone Had Told Me</u>. Kadima Press, 2004. (Grades 8 and up)

    ⁓ Reading this book first can help young adults avoid dangerous situations and possible regrets later on. Ms. Saul shares her life lessons with young adults, including the following topics: Defining Boundaries, Gaining a New Perspective, Expecting the Unexpected, Choices that Change Your Life, Dealing with Failure and Regret, Pain and Suffering as Part of Living, Alcohol and Drug Abuse, Preventing Abuse, Life and Death, You and the World, Relationships, Family and Friends, Forgiveness, and Live Your Dreams.

Seaward, Brian. <u>Hot Stones and Funny Bones : Teens Helping Teens Cope with Stress and Anger</u>. Health Communications, 2002. (Grades 7-12)

    ⁓ Provides an inside look at ways in which teens cope with their stress and anger, such as keeping a journal, meditating, or having a good laugh, and includes advice for parents and other teens.

Shores, Steve. <u>Stressbusters : For Teens Under Pressure</u>. Vine Books, 2002. (Grades 6-12)

    ⁓ Stressbusters is a book to help teens lower their stress level. The first half of the book focuses on showing a teen how to identify and increase the resources they have to reduce stress. And the second half of the book takes a closer look at the stresses teens face and explores how they can manage those demands.

Weill, Sabrina Solin. <u>We're Not Monsters: Teens Speak Out about Teens in Trouble.</u> HarperTempest, 2002. (Grades 8 – 12)

    ⁓ Each chapter offers a variety of the issues including school shootings, anxiety, suicide, self-injury, and sex crimes, facts and statistics, plus advice and the voices of teenagers themselves. Weill also includes suggestions for further reading as well as phone numbers and Web addresses of organizations designed to help.

Attention Defecit / Attention Defecit Hyperactivity Disorder

Dixon, Ellen B. & Nadeau, Kathleen G. Learning to Slow Down and Pay Attention: A Book for Kids About ADD. Magination, 1997. (Grades 6-9)
- This workbook gives kids with ADD the lowdown on such matters as how to clean a room quickly and easily and how to make sure they do their homework on time.

Gehert. I'm Somebody Too. Verbal Images Press, 1992. (Grades 5-8)
- Emily, 12, has a younger brother who is hyperactive and a slow learner. Her worries about him affect her schoolwork and her peer relationships. They learn that the boy has ADD--"Attention Deficit Disorder"--which is treatable through structuring his behavior and taking medication.

Gantos, Jack. Joey Pigza Loses Control. HarperTrophy, 2002. (Grades 6-9)
- Now that Joey has a handle on his actions, he feels prepared to face his estranged father, Carter Pigza. The only problem is that Joey's dad is just as wired as Joey used to be. When Carter flushes his meds, Joey has to decide if being friends with his dad is worth losing his hard-won self-control.

Gantos, Jack. Joey Pigza Swallowed the Key. HarperTrophy, 2000. (Grades 6-9)

~Joey Pigza can't sit still. He can't pay attention, he can't follow the rules, and he can't help it -- especially when his meds aren't working. Joey knows he's really a *good* kid, but no matter how hard he tries to do the right thing, something always seems to go wrong.

Gantos, Jack.   What Would Joey Do.   Farrar, Straus and Giroux, 2002 (Grades 6-9)
~ This book is about a boy named Joey who is dealing with of all his parent's problems. In the final of the Joey trilogy, Joey accepts himself and even finds true love.

Littleman, Ellen, Nadeau, Kathleen, & Quinn, Patricia.   Understanding Girls With AD/HD. Advantage Books, 2000.   (Grades 6 & up).
~ This is a book to read if you suspect a daughter has AD/HD, or if you have AD/HD yourself.   This book is broken down into age groups - preschool, elementary, etc.

Quinn, Patricia.   Putting on the Brakes: Young People's Guide to Understanding Attention Deficit Hyperactivity Disorders (ADHD). Magination, July 2001. (Grades 3-8)
~ When young people learn they have attention deficit hyperactivity disorder (ADHD), they often have many questions, doubts, and fears. This book attempts to address these questions and needs.

Autism/Aspergers Syndrome

Edwards, Michele Engel. <u>Autism</u>. Gale Group, 2001. (Grades 6-10)
- Edwards defines autism and outlines theories of its causes and current treatments. Separate chapters deal with this disorder in children and adults. One chapter describes Asperger's syndrome and the autistic savant, citing stories of famous people.

Lasky, Kathryn. <u>Home Free</u>. Bantam Doubleday Dell Books for Young Readers, 1987. (Grades 7 and up)
- Fifteen-year-old Sam's fight to save a wilderness area for endangered eagles helps an autistic girl return to reality and reveals her strange hidden power

Rosenberg, Marsha Sarah. <u>Everything You Need to Know when a Brother or Sister Is Autistic</u>. The Rosen Publishing Group, Inc., 2000. (Grades 5-9)
- Discusses what autism it, how it is diagnosed and treated, and ways that siblings of people with autism can find support.

Spence, Eleanor. <u>October Child</u>. Oxford University Press, 1976. (Grades 9-12)
- About a child with Autism

Werlin, Nancy. <u>Are You Alone on Purpose?</u> Houghton Mifflin Company, 1994. (Grades 7-12)
- Thirteen-year-old Alison Shandling has always been the good child: calming her autistic twin brother, deflecting her mother's rage, and pleasing her aloof father. Harry Roth has always been the cool kid who tests everyone's limits, especially those of his widowed

father, the town's rabbi. The two dislike each other at first sight. When an accident confines Harry to a wheelchair, Alison recognizes his frustration and loneliness and initiates a friendship.

Williams, James M.   Out to Get Jack. Trafford Publishing, 2003. (Grades 6-12)
- Jack Lack is a mainstreamed eleven-year-old with high-functioning autism. Because he can "talk and did well on spelling tests," he doesn't qualify for the sanctuary of the autism classroom, but instead has been thrown into the BD/JD [behavior-disordered/juvenile delinquent] classroom, which is full of wise-cracking kids. Jack is the only one who doesn't constantly misbehave, but because he lacks social skills, he is the one who is invariably blamed for everyone else's misdeeds.

Blended Families

Bates, Betty. <u>Thatcher Payne-in-the-Neck</u>. Holiday House, 1985.
    (Grades 5-8)
    ~ Kib and Thatcher, long-time friends, get their parents together.
    However, they have second thoughts after the marriage.

Cohn, Rachel. <u>The Steps</u>. Simon & Schuster Children's Publishing, 2003.
    (Grades 6-8)
    ~ *The Steps* is a great realistic fiction about a girl named Annabel.
    She lives in New York City with her Mom and Grandma because her
    parents are divorced. Annabel learns that she has to go visit her Dad,
    who lives in Australia with his wife, Penney, and her disastrous kids,
    Lucy, Angus, and new baby Beatrice.

Craven, Linda. <u>Stepfamilies: New Patterns in Harmony</u>. Messner, 1982.
    (Grades 7-12)
    ~ This book discusses the many types of problems and conflicts that
    arise in step families.

Getzoff, Ann and McClenahan, Carolyn. <u>Stepkids: A Survival Guide for
    Teenagers in Stepfamilies</u>. Walker, 1984. (Grades 7-12)
    ~ This book presents examples of problems in stepfamilies from the
    viewpoint of the teen. It is suggested that older children have the
    power to improve the functioning of the family.

Gleitzman, Morris. <u>Sticky Beak</u>. Bt Bound, 1999. (Grades 4-6)
    ~ Rowena shows her dislike for her step mom by throwing things
    but soon learns to accept/like her situation.

Hathorn, Libby. <u>Thunderwith</u>. Heinemann, 1989. (Grades 4-8)
  - From the moment Gladwyn saw Lara, Lara could sense her disapproval and displeasure. Even after her warm welcome from her future brother and sisters - Garnet, Opal, and Jasper, Lara's desperate attempt to join in the family was shattered by her new sister, Pearl, and her mother, Gladwyn. As Lara struggles to adjust into her new home, she has to also cope with new enemies such as Gowd Gadrey - the school bully who tries to take away the remaining joy in her life.

Leach, Norman. <u>My Wicked Step-Mother</u>. Macmillan, 1993. (Grades 4-8)
  - When his father remarries, Tom has a difficult time accepting his new step-mother.

MacLachlan, Patricia. <u>Sarah Plain and Tall</u>. HarperCollins, 1985. (Grades 5-8)
  - A story about two children, Anna and Caleb, whose lives are changed forever when their widowed papa advertises for a mail-order bride.

Mark, Jan. <u>Trouble Half Way</u>. Lythway, 1990. (Grades 9-12)
  - Events at home shake everything Amy's been planning with gymnastics.

Wolfe, Tobias. <u>The Boy's Life</u>. Grove Press, 2000. (Grades 7-12)
  - Separated by divorce from his father and brother, Toby and his mother are constantly on the move, yet they develop an extraordinarily close, almost telepathic relationship. As Toby fights for identity and self-respect against the unrelenting hostility of a new stepfather, his experiences are meaningful and comical.

Bullying/ridicule

Blume, Judy. <u>Blubber</u>. Pan/Heinemann, 1980.   (Grades   4-8)
   ~ Jill is at school with her friend teasing Linda, who is so fat, it's not
   funny. Everybody at school calls her 'Blubber'. But when everybody
   starts to tease Jill, she finds out how horrible it is to be teased. With
   no one sitting next to her in class or at lunch time, Jill decides that
   she will never ever tease someone again.

Caswell, Brian. <u>Mike</u>. University of Queensland Press, 1993. (Grades 5-8)
   ~ When a twelve-year-old Australian moves with his mother to
   Sydney, he is victimized by a bully at school and befriended by a
   neighbor who has a secret to share.

Cohen-Posey, Kate. <u>How to Handle Bullies, Teasers, and Other Meanies</u>.
   Rainbow Books, 1995. (Grades 3-8).
   ~ A parent-child resource book, *How to Handle Bullies, Teasers and
   Other Meanies* covers annoying name calling, vicious prejudice,
   explosive anger, dangerous situations, and causes of difficult behavior.
   It uses dozens of examples and practice exercises to teach a comic
   approach to handling cruelty.

Drew, Naomi, M.A. <u>The Kids' Guide to Working Out Conflicts How
   to Keep Cool, Stay Safe, and Get Along.</u> Free Spirit Publishing.
   (Grades 4-8)
   ~ Common forms of conflict, the reasons behind conflicts, and
   positive ways to deal with difficult circumstances are addressed.
   Self-tests and exercises are included to help young people discover
   whether they are conflict-solvers or conflict-makers. Drew also

includes tips for bullying, calming down, lessening stress and tension, letting go of anger and resentment, and eliminating put-downs and other hurtful language.

Feig, Paul. <u>Kick Me: Adventures in Adolescence</u>. Three Rivers Press, 2002. (Grades 7-12).
~ Paul Feig takes you in a time machine to a world of bombardment by dodge balls, ill-fated prom dates, hellish school bus rides, and other aspects of public school life that will keep you laughing in recognition.

Gleitzman, Morris. <u>Blabber Mouth</u>. Harcourt, 1995. (Grades 4-8)
~ Rowena Batts has an inborn disability that renders her incapable of speaking. She lives with her good-natured father. She was formerly enrolled in a special school where she grew adept at sign language, but now the girl and her father have moved to a new town, and she attends public school. There, her muteness and her comical surname make her an easy target for the class bully.

Golding, William. <u>Lord of the Flies</u>. Perigee, 1959. (Grades 8-12)
~ This is a classic tale about a group of English schoolboys who are plane-wrecked on a deserted. At first, the stranded boys cooperate, attempting to gather food, make shelters, and maintain signal fires. Overseeing their efforts are Ralph, "the boy with fair hair," and Piggy. Although Ralph tries to impose order and delegate responsibility, there are many in their number who would rather swim, play, or hunt the island's wild pig population. The situation deteriorates as the trappings of civilization continue to fall away, until Ralph discovers that instead of being hunters, he and Piggy have become the hunted.

Hathorn, Libby. <u>Thunderwith</u>. Heinemann, 1989. (Grades 4-8)
~ From the moment Gladwyn saw Lara, Lara could sense her disapproval and displeasure. Even after her warm welcome from her future brother and sisters - Garnet, Opal, and Jasper, Lara's desperate attempt to join in the family was shattered by her new sister, Pearl, and her mother, Gladwyn. As Lara struggles to adjust into her new home, she has to also cope with new enemies such as Gowd Gadrey - the school bully who tries to take away the remaining joy in her life.

Karres, Erika V. Shearin. <u>Mean Chicks, Cliques, and Dirty Tricks: A Real Girl's Guide to Getting Through the Day with Smarts and Style</u>. Adams Media Corporation, 2003. (Grades 6 and up)

~ A guide for coping with girls who are mean to other girls, using the words of teenagers to explore how the meanness can get started, forms it may take, and what can be done to stop it.

Kaufman, Gershen, Raphael, Lev, and Espeland, Pamela. Stick up for Yourself : Every Kid's Guide to Personal Power & Positive Self-Esteem. Free Spirit Publishing, 1999.(Grades 6-10)
~A self-help guide to positive thinking, high self-esteem, and responsible personal power. The book's premise is that all young people can and should be taught the skills necessary to face common issues, such as making choices, liking themselves, and solving problems. Exercises guide readers through learning about their own feelings, dreams, and needs--while stressing that they are responsible for their own behavior and happiness.

Klein, Robin. Boss of the Pool. Penguin USA, 1992. (Grades 5-8)
~ Shelley, who thinks the world should revolve around her, is upset when her mom takes a job at a home for mentally and physically handicapped children. In this story, Shelley teaches a boy with Downs Syndrome how to swim. Shelley finds herself, and is enlightened by what a great person her mom is. Shelley goes through a great change.

Korman, Gordan. Sixth Grade Nickname Game. Hyperion, 2000. (Grades 5-8)
~ This book is about two boys who love to give nicknames to kids in their class. But when Cassandra arrives, they're at a loss for names. Soon they start to like her and they want her to invite them to a dance. Jeff and Wiley, who never fought together, started to fight over her.

Lubar, David. Hidden Talents. Starscape, 2003. (Grades 7 and up)
~ Martin and his friends start to believe all the negative things people say about them until they discover their hidden talents.

McPhee, Peter. New Blood. James Lorimer and Company, 2007. (Grades 9 and up)
~ After moving from a negative school experience, Paul learns to deal with and recover from bullying. He is also able to find new hope.

Romain, Trevor and Verdick, Elizabeth. Bullies Are a Pain in the Brain. Free Spirit Publishing, 1997. (Grades 6-8)
~ Every child needs to know how to cope with bullies, and this book blends humor with serious, practical suggestions that will help kids understand, avoid and stand up to bullies while preserving their own self-esteem.

Saul, Laya. <u>You Don't Have to Learn Everything the Hard Way: What I Wish Someone Had Told Me</u>. Kadima Press, 2004. (Grades 8 and up)
~ Reading this book first can help young adults avoid dangerous situations and possible regrets later on. Ms. Saul shares her life lessons with young adults, including the following topics: Defining Boundaries, Gaining a New Perspective, Expecting the Unexpected, Choices that Change Your Life, Dealing with Failure and Regret, Pain and Suffering as Part of Living, Alcohol and Drug Abuse, Preventing Abuse, Life and Death, You and the World, Relationships, Family and Friends, Forgiveness, and Live Your Dreams.

Simmons, Rachel. <u>Odd Girl Out: The Hidden Culture of Aggression in Girls</u>. Harcourt Brace & Company, 2003. (Grades 9 and up)
~ Why are girls becoming more aggressive in their everyday lives, and how is it affecting their overall self-esteem? Rachel Simmons, a Rhodes scholar who has painstakingly researched female bullying and the psychology of girls, feels that girls' aggressiveness is just as harmful as that of boys but is much harder to recognize.

Spinelli, Jerry. <u>Loser</u>. HarperTrophy, 2003. (Grades 5-8)
~ Loser is the story of 6th grader, Donald Zinkoff. His love of, but lack of skill, in school among many other aspects of life are just now starting to be noticed by his peers. Though he hasn't changed over the years, Donald has now become the outcast.

Cancer

Ackermann, Adrienne & Ackermann, Abigail. <u>Our Mom has Cancer</u>.
American Cancer Society, 2001. (Grades 5-8)
- Two sisters, ages eleven and thirteen, describe what it was like
for them when their mother was diagnosed with breast cancer and
underwent surgery and chemotherapy

Amadeo, D.M. <u>There's a Little Bit of Me in Jamey</u>. Whitman & Co, 1989.
(Grades 5-8)
- Brian, whose younger brother Jamey has leukemia, feels frightened,
confused, and neglected by his parents; but he finds some comfort
when he donates bone marrow to his brother.

Armstrong, Lance. <u>It's Not About the Bike</u>. Berkley Trade, 2001. (Grades
7 and up)
- Lance Armstrong discusses his successes in life and overcoming
testicular cancer even when he was told he'd never ride again.

Beckman, Gunnel. <u>Admission to the Feast</u>. Holt, Rinehart and Winston,
1972. (Grades 9-12)
- A nineteen-year-old girl, dying of leukemia, writes a long letter to
a friend in an attempt to stabilize her crumbling world.

Brashares, Ann. <u>Sisterhood of the Traveling Pants</u>. Dell Books for Young
Readers, 2005. (Grades 7 and up)
- The story of four very different friends who spend their summer
apart. Each faces their own issues, but is comforted by the arrival

of their thrift store jeans that magically fit everyone. Issues include having a friend with leukemia, relationship pressures, divorce, and family pressures.

Carney, Karen L. <u>What is Cancer Anyway?: Explaining Cancer to Children of All Ages.</u> Dragonfly Pub, 1998. (Grades K and up)
~ Explains cancer to children of all ages

Coerr, Eleanor. <u>Sadako and the Thousand paper Cranes</u>. Turtleback Books, 1977.(Grades 5-8)
~ Sadako Sasaki was just two when the atom bomb was dropped on her home city of Hiroshima. Ten years later she developed leukemia. Facing long days in bed, Sadako spent the time folding paper cranes, for the legend holds that if a sick person folds 1,000, the gods will make her well again.

Gleitzman, Morris. <u>Two Weeks With Queen</u>. HarperTrophy, 1993. (Grades 7-12)
~ Colin, who was once self-centered, matures rapidly as his brother is diagnosed with cancer and he finds an unlikely friend whose partner is dying from AIDS.

Gunther, John. <u>Death Be Not Proud</u>. Perennial, 1998. (Grades 9-12)
~ This true story relates a father's recollection of his son's courageous and spirited battle against the brain tumor that would take his life at the age of seventeen.

Lowry, Lois. <u>Summer to Die</u>. Laurel Leaf, 1984. (Grades 7-12)
~ Thirteen-year-old Meg envies her sister's beauty and popularity. Her feelings don't make it any easier for her to cope with Molly's strange illness and eventual death from leukemia.

Lund, Doris. <u>Eric</u>. Lippincott, 1974. (Grades 8-12)
~ Eric was seventeen when he heard the doctor's verdict about the disease that wanted his life. At first he and his family could not believe it. Eric was the picture of everything a youth should be--a champion athlete, a splendid human being, vibrant with energy and loved by all who knew him. Eric had to do as much as was humanly possible. But if the odds were not good, they were good enough for Eric. Given the choice between life and death, Eric chose to live. This story is told by Eric's mother.

Martin, Carrie and Martin, Chia. <u>The Rainbow of Feelings of Cancer: A Book for Children Who Have a Loved One With Cancer</u>. Hohm Press, 2001. (Grades 6 & up)

~ Children need to share their feelings and ask questions, especially in stressful times. This book encourages conversation between children and those who love them

McDaniel, Lurlene. <u>Always and Forever</u>. Laurel Leaf, 2004. (Grades 7 and up)
~ 16-year old Melissa has it all. . . until she's diagnosed with cancer.

McDaniel, Lurlene. <u>Garden of Angels</u>. Delacorte Books for Young Readers, 2003. (Grades 7 and up)
~ 14 year old Darcy finds comfort in her mother's garden when her mother is going through a struggle with breast cancer.

McDaniel, Lurlene. <u>Goodbye Doesn't Mean Forever</u>. Bantam, 1989. (Grades 7 and up)
~ This is the sequel to <u>Too Young To Die</u>. <u>Goodbye Doesn't Mean Forever</u> is about two best friends, Jory and Melissa, and about Melissa fight with leukemia. Jory stuck with Melissa until the very end.

McDaniel, Lurlene. <u>No Time To Cry</u>. Bantam, 1996. (Grades 7 and up)
~ Dawn Rochelle has overcome cancer and chemotherapy. Now she struggles as she tries to get back to life as a normal teenager.

McDaniel, Lurlene. <u>Now I Lay Me Down to Sleep</u>. Bantam, 1991. (Grades 6-9)
~ Carrie is a 15-year old who was diagnosed with leukemia 3 years ago. Along with her disease, Carrie also deals with the divorce of her parents. She meets Keith, who helps her keep going, at a support group for cancer survivors.

McDaniel, Lurlene. <u>The Time Capsule</u>. Delacorte Books for Young Readers, 2003. (Grades 7 and up)
~ Twin siblings have great hopes and dreams until one of them is diagnosed with cancer. When Adam gets sick for a second time, it's bitter-sweet as the illness reunites the family.

McDaniel, Lurlene. <u>Too Young to Die</u>. Starfire, 1989. (Grades 7 and up)
~ Melissa receives devastating news about her health. At first she refuses to accept the doctor's diagnosis of leukemia, but as her illness gets worse she cannot deny the truth. The caring and closeness Melissa feels toward her family   and especially toward Jory help her find the inner strength and courage to face the mysteries of living and dying.

Murray, G., & Jampolsky, <u>Straight From the Siblings: Another Look at the Rainbow</u>. Celestial Arts, 1983. (Grades 4-12)

~ A group of thirty-four children share their experiences with terminally ill brothers and sisters.

Strasser, Todd. <u>Friends Till the End</u>. Laurel Leaf Books, 1981. (Grades 6-12)

~ David befriended a nerd and has to deal with peer pressure as he supports his new friend throughout his agonizing struggle with leukemia.

Child Abuse

D'Amosio, Richard. No Language But a Cry. Doubleday, 1970. (Grades 9 and up)
- This is the true story of Dr. D'Ambrosio's struggle to help a battered child who has never spoken a word because of the physical abuse inflicted by her parents.

Dolan, Edward. Child Abuse. Watts, 1980. (Grades 7-12)
- The principle areas of child abuse, including physical and sexual abuse, are outlined.

Draper, Sharon. Forged By Fire. Simon Pulse, 1998. (Grades 6-12)
- This prequel to Draper's Tears of a Tiger tells of a young man struggling to protect his little sister from a drug-addicted mother and an abusive father.

Haskins, James. The Child Abuse Help Book. Niles, Albert Whitman, 1981. (Grades 5-9)
- The problems that lead to and stem from child abuse accompany directions for help, including suggestions for personal action

Hyde, Margaret. Cry Softly: The Story of Child Abuse. Westminster, 1980. (Grades 7 and up)
- Discusses child abuse, its history in England and America, ways to prevent and stop it, and how to report suspected cases.

Kellogg, Majorie. Like the Lion's Tooth. Farrar, Straus, and Giroux, 1972. (Grades 5-9)

⁓ Eleven year old Ben, who has been physically and sexually abused by his father, is sent to school for "problem children." Ben eventually resigns himself to the situation.

Klass, David. You Don't Know Me. HarperTempest, 2002. (Grades 7 and up)
⁓ A 14-year-old describes the physical and emotional abuse from his mother's boyfriend. "The hero's underlying sense of isolation and thread of hope will strike a chord with nearly every adolescent" (Reed Business Information, Inc, 2002).

Mazer, Harry. The War on Villa Street. Delacort, 1978. (Grades 5-9)
⁓ Willis, an eight year old, is frequently beaten by his alcoholic father. After striking back at his father, Willis runs away but returns, hoping things will improve.

Pelzer, David. A Child Called "It". Health Communications, 1995. (Grades 7 & up).
⁓ Pelzer describes the true story of how he was beaten by his mother and what steps were taken to overcome the abuse.

Pelzer, David. Help Yourself: Finding Hope, Courage, and Happiness. Plume, 2001. (Grades 7 & up).
⁓ Explains how to move on after painful abuse.

Pelzer, David. Lost Boy. Health Communications, 1997. (Grades 7 & up).
⁓ This true story about the author describes various foster homes and challenges David faced after he was abused by his mother.

Pledge, Deanna S., Ph.D. When Something Feels Wrong A Survival Guide About Abuse for Young People. Free Spirit Publishing. (Grades 7 and up)
⁓ When Something Feels Wrong reassures young adults with a history of being abused. Pledge includes checklists and journaling ideas to help readers to explore their feelings and experiences. There are also real life examples to show readers they're not alone.

Staff, Handprint. What Jamie Saw. Hand Print, 1991. (Grades 6-9)
⁓ Jamie witnessed his baby sister being tossed across the room. He is relieved when his mother witnesses the abuse and they escape.

Childhood Remembered

Agee, James. <u>A Death in the Family.</u> Vintage, 1998. (Grades 9-12)
- Through a family member's death, we see a novel of innocence, tenderness, and loss.

Alcott, Louisa May. <u>Little Women.</u> Penguin, 1989. (Grades 3 & up)
- The story of the March girls' journey to adulthood

Alcott, Louisa May. <u>Little Men.</u> Signet, 1993. (Grades 3 & up)
- The sequel to Little Women, this story continues the story of Jo March, who goes on to get married and inherit an estate with which she creates an experimental school for boys.

Angelou, May. <u>I Know Why the Caged Bird Sings</u>. Bantam, 1983. (Grades 9-12)
- This memoir traces Maya Angelou's childhood in a small, rural community during the 1930s. It also recognizes the dignity and courage of black men and women.

Cather, Willa. <u>My Antonia.</u> Mariner Books, 1995. (Grades 9 & up)
- My Antonia focuses on the hard life of the pioneer woman on the prairie. Werevisit the immigrant life in the Nebraska heartland.

Llewellyn, Richard. <u>How Green Was My Valley</u>. Scribner, 1997. (Grades 9 & up)
- Llewellyn's tale of a young man's coming-of-age in a small Welsh mining town.

Parks, Gordon. <u>The Learning Tree</u>. Fawcett Books, 1987. (Grades 7 & up)

- This is the story of a black family as they struggle to understand and accept thechallenge of their special world.

Saul, Laya. <u>You Don't Have to Learn Everything the Hard Way: What I Wish Someone Had Told Me</u>. Kadima Press, 2004. (Grades 8 and up)
- Reading this book first can help young adults avoid dangerous situations and possible regrets later on. Ms. Saul shares her life lessons with young adults, including the following topics: Defining Boundaries, Gaining a New Perspective, Expecting the Unexpected, Choices that Change Your Life, Dealing with Failure and Regret, Pain and Suffering as Part of Living, Alcohol and Drug Abuse, Preventing Abuse, Life and Death, You and the World, Relationships, Family and Friends, Forgiveness, and Live Your Dreams.

Wilder, Thorton. <u>Our Town</u>. Perennial, 1998. (Grades 9 & up)
- All about the drama of life in the small village of Grover's Corners

Williams, Tennessee. <u>The Glass Menagerie</u>. New Directions Publishing, 1999. (Grades 9 & up)
- The story of a family whose lives form a triangle of quiet desperation

Conflict/Conflict Resolution

Cohen-Posey, Kate. How to Handle Bullies, Teasers, and Other Meanies.
Rainbow Books, 1995. (Grades 3-8).
~ A parent-child resource book, *How to Handle Bullies, Teasers and Other Meanies* covers annoying name calling, vicious prejudice, explosive anger, dangerous situations, and causes of difficult behavior. It uses dozens of examples and practice exercises to teach a comic approach to handling cruelty.

Cohen-Sandler, Roni and Silver, Michelle. I'm Not Mad, I Just Hate You!: A New Understanding of Mother-Daughter Conflict. Penguin, 2000. (Grades 9 and up)
~ Teen girls, who are socialized to stifle their anger and avoid confrontation, frequently take out their frustration on their mothers as the only safe and available targets. *I'm Not Mad, I Just Hate You!* combines the expertise of a clinical psychologist (who has worked with women and adolescent girls for more than twenty years) with that of a senior editor at a leading teen magazine. The book demonstrates how mother-daughter friction during adolescence, managed creatively, empowers girls by teaching them invaluable skills and can even foster intimacy.

Drew, Naomi, M.A. The Kids' Guide to Working Out Conflicts How to Keep Cool, Stay Safe, and Get Along. Free Spirit Publishing. (Grades 4-8)
~ Common forms of conflict, the reasons behind conflicts, and positive ways to   deal with difficult circumstances are addressed. Self-tests and exercises are   included to help young people discover

whether they are conflict-solvers or conflict-makers. Drew also includes tips for bullying, calming down, lessening stress and tension, letting go of anger and resentment, and eliminating put-downs and other hurtful language.

McCoy, Kathy, and Wibbelsman, Charles, M.D. <u>Life Happens: A Teenager's Guide to Friends, Failure, Sexuality, Love, Rejection, Addiction, Peer Pressure, Families, Loss, Depression, Change, and Other challenges.</u> Berkley Publishing, 1996. (Grades 7-12)
~ Offers advice on how to cope with such feelings as sadness, anger, and anxiety related to various problems including the death of a family member, teen pregnancy, the end of a romantic relationship, being homosexual, and having an alcoholic parent.

Packer, Alex J., Ph.D. <u>Bringing Up Parents The Teenager's Handbook.</u> Free Spirit Press. (Grades 7-12).
~ Includes suggestions on how teens can resolve conflicts with parents, improve family relationships, earn trust, accept responsibility, and help to create a healthier, happier home environment.

Saul, Laya. <u>You Don't Have to Learn Everything the Hard Way: What I Wish Someone Had Told Me</u>. Kadima Press, 2004. (Grades 8 and up)
~ Reading this book first can help young adults avoid dangerous situations and possible regrets later on. Ms. Saul shares her life lessons with young adults, including the following topics: Defining Boundaries, Gaining a New Perspective, Expecting the Unexpected, Choices that Change Your Life, Dealing with Failure and Regret, Pain and Suffering as Part of Living, Alcohol and Drug Abuse, Preventing Abuse, Life and Death, You and the World, Relationships, Family and Friends, Forgiveness, and Live Your Dreams.

Wojno, Mary Ann Burkley. My <u>Life My Choices: Key Issues for Young Adults</u>. Paulist Press, 1996. (Grades 7 and up)
~ From students' perspectives: students write about the issues they deal with.

Death ~ General

Alexander, Sue. <u>Nadia the Willful</u>. Pantheon Books, 1993. (Grades 3-6)
    ~ When her favorite brother disappears in the desert forever, Nadia refuses to let him be forgotten, despite her father's bitter decree that his name shall not be uttered.

Babbitt, Natalie. <u>Tuck Everlasting</u>. Farrar Straus & Giroux, 1985. (Grades 6-12)
    ~ The Tuck family discovers a spring which grants eternal life, decides to protect it for the sake of humanity, and finally meets challenges to their goals in the form of a ten-year-old's inquisitive mind and a greedy stranger who suspects their secret.

Beckman, Gunnel. <u>Admission to the Feast</u>. Holt, Rinehart and Winston, 1972. (Grades 9-12)
    ~ A nineteen-year-old girl, dying of leukemia, writes a long letter to a friend in an attempt to stabilize her crumbling world.

Craven, Margaret. <u>I Heard the Owl Call My Name</u>. Laurel Leaf, 1980. (Grades 7-12)
    ~ Tells of a young vicar named Mark, sent to a remote Kwakiutl village not knowing he has less than three years to live.

Forrai, Maria S. <u>A Look at Death</u>. Lerner, 1978. (Grades 1-6)
    ~ Text and photographs present the concept of death, the importance of grief, and the customs of mourning.

Grieve, James. <u>Season of Grannies</u>. University of Queensland Press. (Grades 9-12)

~ When Jacqui turns sixteen, she is faced with an older a couple who plan to practice euthansia.

Saul, Laya. <u>You Don't Have to Learn Everything the Hard Way: What I Wish Someone Had Told Me</u>. Kadima Press, 2004. (Grades 8 and up)

~ Reading this book first can help young adults avoid dangerous situations and possible regrets later on. Ms. Saul shares her life lessons with young adults, including the following topics: Defining Boundaries, Gaining a New Perspective, Expecting the Unexpected, Choices that Change Your Life, Dealing with Failure and Regret, Pain and Suffering as Part of Living, Alcohol and Drug Abuse, Preventing Abuse, Life and Death, You and the World, Relationships, Family and Friends, Forgiveness, and Live Your Dreams.

Death - of A Friend

Bauer, Marion D. <u>On My Honor</u>. Yearling Books, 1987. (Grades 5-9)
    ~ Twelve-year-old Joel has unwillingly agreed to bike out to the state park with his daredevil friend Tony. "On his honor," he promises his father to be careful, knowing that Tony wants them to climb the dangerous park bluffs. When they arrive, however, Tony abruptly changes his mind and heads for the river. With his promise jangling in his mind, Joel follows Tony in for a swim. Tony drowns in the dirty, turbulent water, leaving Joel to face his guilty conscience, and his father, alone....

Carlstrom, Nancy. <u>Blow Me a Kiss, Miss Lilly</u>. Harper and Row, 1990. (Grades K-3)
    ~ When her best friend, an old lady dies, Sara learns that the memory of a loved one never dies.

Clardy, Andrea Fleck. <u>Dusty Was My Friend</u>. Human Sciences Press, 1985. (Grades 5-9)
    ~ Eight-year-old Benjamin remembers his friend Dusty, who was killed in a car accident, and tries to understand his own feelings about losing a friend in this way.

Cohn, Janice. <u>I Had a Friend Named Peter</u>. Morrow, 1987. (Grades 2-8)
    ~ When Betsy learns about the death of her friend, her parents and her teacher help her answer her questions about dying and the funeral process.

Draper, Sharon. <u>Tears of a Tiger</u>. Simon Pulse, 1996. (Grades 6-12)

⁓ A high school basketball star struggles with guilt and depression following the drunk-driving accident that killed his best friend. Short chapters and alternating view points provide "raw energy and intense emotion," said Publishers Weekly.

Draper, Sharon. Forged by Fire. Atheneum, 1997. (Grades 7 and up)
⁓ Deals with the following issues: tough social issues, such as child abuse, drug addiction, incest, bulimia, and domestic violence, the death of a close friend, and a drunk, evil stepfather trying to sexually assault his younger stepsister.

Gootman, Marilyn E., Ed.D. When a Friend Dies. Free Spirit Publishing. (Grades 5 and up)
⁓ With a foreward by REM lead singer Michael Stipe, this book answers questions grieving teens often have, such as: "How should I be acting?" "Is it wrong to go to parties and have fun?" and "What if I can't handle my grief on my own?"

Miklowitz, Gloria. Goodbye Tomorrow. Delacorte Books for Young Readers, 1987.(Grades 9-12)
⁓ Alex, popular athlete and the lover of beautiful blonde Shannon, begins to have problems with his immune system a year after he had blood transfusions following a car crash.

Orr, Wendy. Leaving it to You. Angus & Robertson. (Grades 6-12)
⁓ Deals with the death of an elderly friend

Paterson, Katherine. Bridge to Terabitha. Crowell, 1977. (Grades 3-8)
⁓ A ten year old boy whose life is enhanced by a newcomer has to deal with her sudden death.

Smith, Doris Buchanan. A Taste of Blackberries. Crowell, 1973. (Grades 4 & up)
⁓ A young boy recounts his efforts to adjust to the sudden death of his best friend.

Death - of A Family Member

Adler, C.S. Daddy's Climbing Tree. Clarion, 1993. (Grades 4 & up)
  ~ Jessica refuses to believe that her father died when he is killed in a hit-and-run accident.

Aliki. The Two of Them. Greenwillow, 1979. (Grades K-5)
  ~ A grandfather and a little girl look after one another from the day she is born until the day he dies.

Anderson, Laurie Halse. Catalyst. Speak, 2003. (Grades 9 and up)
  ~ This story is about a girl named Kate. She desperately wants to get in to one specific college. When she's rejected, her whole life seems to crumble. As a passionate runner, she can't outrun the pain of being rejected. . . or the pain that really still haunts her – her mother's death.

Anderson, Susan. The Journey from Abandonment to Healing. Berkley Publishing Group, 2000. (Grades 9 and up)
  ~ Anderson's book defines the five phases of a different kind of grieving—grieving over a lost relationship. *The Journey From Abandonment to Healing* is designed to help all victims of emotional breakups--whether they are suffering from a recent loss, or a lingering wound from the past; whether they are caught up in patterns that sabotage their own relationships, or they're in a relationship where they no longer feel loved.

Buck, Pearl S. Big Wave. Harper Collins Juvenile Books, 1973. (Grades 5-8)
  ~ His family and village were swept away by a tidal wave. Jiya learns to live with the ever-present dangers from the sea and volcano.

Carmody, Isobelle. Greylands. Penguin Books Australia Ltd. (Grades 9-12)
~ Jack and his younger sister Ellen struggle to survive emotionally after the death of their mother, made worse by the complete withdrawal of their father. Greylands is a story of grief and recognition of children's emotions, especially the grief and guilt a child experiences after a parent's suicide.

Cohn, Janice. Molly's Rosebush. Whitman, 1994. (Grades K-4)
~ When the new baby isn't strong enough to be born, Molly and her family findways to express their feelings and comfort each other.

Couloumbis, Audrey. Getting Near to Baby. Penguin Putnam Books for Young Readers, 2001. (Grades 6-8)
~ Getting Near to Baby is a tragedy about Willa Jo (who is 12 years old) and her Little sister (7 years old). Little Sister stopped talking after her baby sister died from drinking bad water. This is about a family getting over a tragedy.

Creech, Sharon. Pleasing the Ghost. Harpercollins Juvenile Books, 1996. (Grades 5 & up)
~ Nine year old Dennis, whose uncle and father have both recently died, is visited by his uncle Arvie's ghost, and together, they take care of some unfinished business.

Deuker, Carl. Heart of a Champion. HarperTeen, 1994. (Grades 6-10)
~ Seth still hasn't come to terms with the death of his father 5 years prior. He meet Jimmy though baseball. Jimmy is dealing with his parents' divorce and he becomes an alcoholic himself. When Seth has to deal with the death of a friend on top of it all, baseball and the support of his mom are what seems to get him through.

Gleitzman, Morris. Two Weeks with the Queen. Galaxy, 2002. (Grades 5-12)
~ After the sudden diagnosis of his younger brother's cancer, Colin is sent from his home in Australia to relatives in England. Once there, he tries to contact a number of institutions--including the Queen--in order to obtain the best possible medical assistance for his brother. He fails in these efforts, but eventually receives some help and understanding from a homosexual couple--one of whom has AIDS.

Greene, Constance. Beat the Turtle Drum. Viking, 1976. (Grades 5-8)
~ A young girl learns to cope with her feelings after the accidental death of her sister.

Guest, Elissa. <u>Over the Moon</u>. Starfire, 1987. (Grades 9-12)
- A story about a girl who must rebuild her life after the sudden death of her parents.

Gunther, John. <u>Death Be Not Proud</u>. Perennial, 1998. Grades 9-12
- This true story relates a father's recollection of his son's courageous and spirited battle against the brain tumor that would take his life at the age of seventeen.

Hambrook, Diane. <u>A Mother Loss Workbook: Healing Exercises for Daughters</u>. Perennial, 1997. (Grades 6 and up)
- A Mother Loss Workbook is designed to help the motherless daughter tell the story she needs to tell--her story. Its varied exercises provide both careful direction and room for self-expression. This book is a safe place where no one will judge a woman, where the work she must do can be done in her own time, at her own pace, and at any stage of mourning.

Hill, Deidre. <u>Flight From Fear</u>. Hodder & Stoughton Childrens Division, 1989. (Grades 9-12)
- It is 1942. Tommy Hooper's mother and sister have been killed in the Blitz and Tommy is sent to an Australian country town to live with his aunt. He does not fit in and feels miserable.

Hilton, Nette. <u>Web</u>. HarperCollinsPublishers, 1998. (Grades 5-8)
- Deals with the death of a Grandparent

Hinton, S.E. <u>The Outsiders</u>. Prentice Hall, 1997. (Grades 7-12)
- According to Ponyboy, there are two kinds of people in the world: one has money, can get away with just about anything, and the other always lives on the outside and needs to watch his back. Ponyboy learns how to live as a greaser in a family whose parents have passed away.

Hoffman, Alice. <u>Green Angel</u>. Scholastic Press, 2003. (Grades 9 and up)
- When her whole family is killed in a fire, 15 year old Green relies on spirits to help her heal.

Jukes, Mavies. <u>Blackberries in the Dark</u>. Alfred P. Knopf, 1983. (Grades 2-6)
- The story of a boy visiting his grandmother after his grandfather's death

Jukes, Mavis. <u>I'll See You In My Dreams</u>. Knopf, 1992. (Grades 3-8)
- A girl, preparing to visit her seriously ill uncle, imagines being a sky-writer, flying over his bed with a message of love.

Kelleher, Victor. <u>Del-Del</u>. Random House, 1993. (Grades 9-12)
  - A teenage girl in Sydney, Australia, records how her family is devastated by her older sister's death and by the bizarre behavior of her gifted younger brother, who seems to be cold and unfeeling.

Krementz, Jill. <u>How it Feels When a Parent Dies</u>. Knopf, 1981. (Grades 5-12)
  - Eighteen young people ranging in age from seven to sixteen discuss the questions, fears, and bereavement they experience when one of their parents dies.

Lowry, Lois. <u>Summer to Die</u>. Laurel Leaf, 1983. (Grades 7-12)
  - Thirteen-year-old Meg envies her sister Molly's beauty and popularity, and these feelings make it difficult for her to cope with Molly's illness and death.

MacLachlan, Patricia. <u>Sarah Plain and Tall</u>. HarperCollins, 1985. (Grades 5-8)
  - A story about two children, Anna and Caleb, whose lives are changed forever when their widowed papa advertises for a mail-order bride.

Mahy, Margaret. <u>Memory</u>. ABC-CLIO, 1989. (Grades 7 & up)
  - On the fifth anniversary of his sister's death, nineteen-year-old Jonny Dart is still troubled by guilt and an imperfect memory of the accident that took her life. He goes searching for answers and closure.

Masson, Sophie. <u>Sooner or Later</u>. University of Queensland Press,1991. (Grades 9-12)
  - When she comes to live with her father in a small Australian town, fifteen-year-old Scilla must deal with her shortcomings, with her grandmother's terminal illness, and with growing racial tensions.

Mazer, Harry. <u>When the Phone Rang</u>. Bt Bound, 1999. (Grades 7-12)
  - After a detached voice on the phone announces the death of their parents in an airplane explosion, the lives of the three Keller children (Lori, 12; Billy, 16; and Kevin, 21) quickly deteriorate into chaos. Well-meaning relatives attempt to split them up, but at Billy's insistence Kevin moves back home so that the three survivors can remain a family unit.

McCoy, Kathy, and Wibbelsman, Charles, M.D. <u>Life Happens: A Teenager's Guide to Friends, Failure, Sexuality, Love, Rejection, Addiction, Peer Pressure, Families, Loss, Depression, Change, and Other challenges</u>. Berkley Publishing, 1996. (Grades 7-12)

~ Offers advice on how to cope with such feelings as sadness, anger, and anxiety related to various problems including the death of a family member, teen pregnancy, the end of a romantic relationship, being homosexual, and having an alcoholic parent.

McDaniel, Lurlene. The Girl Death Left Behind. Laurel Leaf, 1999. (Grades 6-9)
~ At age 14, Beth has to deal with losing her entire family in a car accident.

Miles, Miska. Annie and the Old One. Little Brown and Co.: Boston, 1971. (Grades 4-8)
~ Annie, an Indian child, resorts to extremes in trying to prevent her dear grandmother from dying. The "old one" has said she will return to Earth when she has finished helping Annie and Annie's mother to weave their new rug, so the child does everything she can to delay the project. When the grandmother explains her beliefs, Annie understands and no longer attempts to hold back time.

Murray, G., & Jampolsky, Straight From the Siblings: Another Look at the Rainbow. Celestial Arts, 1983. (Grades 4-12)
~ A group of thirty-four children share their experiences with terminally ill brothers and sisters.

Pershall, Mary. You Take the High Road. Penguin, 1990. (Grades 7-12)
~ Samantha's mother has a baby, Nicholas, whose birth creates some unrest in an already uncomfortable family situation, and whose death by drowning at age two causes the family to fall apart.

Philbrick, Rodman. Young Man And The Sea. Blue Sky Press, 2004. (Grade 5-8)
~ A story of Skiff, who loses his mother and feels responsible for pulling the family back together again.

Sharp, Donna. Blue Days. Macmillan Education Australia Pty Ltd, 1989. (Grades 8-12)
~ A sixteen-year-old wonders whether it's worth growing up at all as she tries to cope with loss, disillusionment, and confusion.

Shelley, Noreen. Faces in a Looking Glass. Oxford University Press, 1974. (Grades 9-12)
~ Deals with the death of a mother

Warner, Sally. This Isn't About the Money. Viking Books, 2002. (Grades 5-8)

~ 12 year old Janey and her sister become orphans when the car they're riding in is hit by a drunk driver. She struggles to keep her parents' spirit alive by trying to convince her new guardians (her grandpa and great aunt), that her parents' memories are worth more than the lawsuit. Eventually, Janey and her sister find a new kind of love from their foster parents.

Woodson, Jacqueline. <u>Miracle's Boys</u>. Speak, 2001. (Grades 9-12)
~ Ty'ree, Charlie, and Lafayette, three brothers must raise themselves after losing both of their parents. The oldest boy gives up his dreams to help raise the younger two who are struggling to find the right path in life. They survive using the strongest bond of all – family.

Depression

Carter, Sharon & Lawrence, Clayton. <u>Coping with Depression</u>. Rosen, 1995. (Grades 7-12)
    - Discusses the different types of depression and ways in which they can be manifested, their possible causes, and ways of dealing with the situation.

Cobain, Bev, R.N., C. <u>When Nothing Matters Anymore A Survival Guide for Depressed Teens.</u> Free Spirit Publishing. (Grades 7 and up)
    - Written by the cousin of Curt Cobain, this book defines and explains adolescent depression, reveals how common it is, describes the symptoms, and how it is treated. Stories and poetry come directly from those who've been affected by depression.

Cronkite, Kathy. <u>On the Edge of Darkness: America's Most Celebrated Actors, Journalists and Politicians Chronicle Their Most Arduous Journey</u>. Delta; July 1, 1995. (Grades 9 & up)
    - Famous people tell of their struggles with depression outside of the spotlight.

Guest, Judith. <u>Ordinary People</u>. Penguin Books, 1993. (Grades 9-12)
    - Seventeen-year-old Conrad Jarrett returns to his parents' home and tries to build a new life for himself after spending eight months in a mental institution for attempted suicide.

Kaysen, Susanna. <u>Girl Interrupted</u>. Random, 1993. (Grades 8-12)
    - In the late 1960s, the author spent nearly two years on the ward for teenage girls at McLean Hospital, a psychiatric facility. Her memoir encompasses vivid portraits of her fellow patients and their keepers.

Luciani, Joseph. <u>Self-Coaching: How to Heal Anxiety and Depression</u>.
    Wiley, 2001. Grades 9 and up
    ~ *Self-Coaching* will show you how to: develop a fresh way of
    thinking, leading to a healthy, adaptive way of living, follow winning
    strategies so you can accomplish what you want in life, use the self-
    talk technique to coach yourself back to health.

McCormick, Patricia. <u>Cut</u>. Scholastic, 2002. (Grades 7-12)
    ~ Deals with mental illness. Teens will relate to the adolescent
    drama and all-important friends as the main character tries to "cut."
    Its readers will find hope in the uplifting end.

Thompson, Tracy. <u>The Beast: A Reckoning with Depression</u>. NAL: Dutton,
    1996. (Grades 9 & up)
    ~ A reporter for *The Washington Post* describes her life-long struggle
    with depression, recounting her painful efforts to comprehend and
    treat her illness.

On Being Labeled "Different"

Drew, Naomi. <u>Kids' Guide to Working out Conflicts: How to Keep Cool, Stay Safe, and Get Along</u>. Free Spirit Publishing, Inc., 2004. (Grades 5-10)
Describes common forms of conflict, the reasons behind conflicts, and various positive ways to deal with and defuse tough situations at school, at home, and in the community without getting physical.

Gleeson, Libby. <u>Dodger</u>. Turton & Chambers Ltd, 1991. (Grades 6-12)
~ Mick, thought of as "a boy that will only let you down," is given the chance to play the Artful Dodger in a school production of "Oliver". The book which reveals the events of his life that led to a memorable crisis is interwoven with letters that his teacher writes describing Mick's progress

Hahn, Mary Downing. <u>Daphne's Book</u>. HarperTrophy, 1996. (Grades 4-7)
~ Daphne is continuously made fun of, but finally shares a terrible secret with Jessica.

Paulsen, Gary. <u>Dancing Carl</u>. Puffin Books, 1983. (Grades 6-8)
~ A remembrance of a man, perceived as "odd," who had a great impact on the lives of two twelve year olds.

Diabetes

Ballard, Carol. <u>Special Diets and Food Allergies</u>. Heinemann, 2006. (Grades 6 and up)
- Ballard answers questions about lactose intolerance, diet and diabetes, weight, food intolerance, and more. This book also explains how some people's bodies react to certain foods and how to manage that.

Christopher, Matt. <u>Shoot for the Hoop</u>. Little, Brown and Company, 1995. (Grades 3-6)
- Rusty's parents want him to stay off the court because of his diabetes. Will his own determination be enough to conquer his disease?

Dominick, Andie. <u>Needles: A Memoir of Growing Up with Diabetes</u>. Simon & Schuster Adult Publishing Group, 2000. (Grades 7 and up)
- Dominick shares her real life story of growing up with diabetes. Her accounts help young adults realize they are not alone.

Loy, Bo Namyth and Loy, Spike Nasmyth. <u>487 Really Cool Tips for Kids with Diabetes</u>. American Diabetes Association, 2003. (Grades 6-12)
- The authors, diagnosed at ages 6 and 7, have lived with diabetes for over 15 years. In this book, they share tips for dealing with diabetes.

Nicholson, Lorna Schultz. <u>Interference</u>. Lorimer, James & Company, Limited, 2004. (Grades 6 and up)

- Josh has worked hard to make it to the elite hockey league. Just when he's found success, he is having a hard time functioning, feeling tired, sluggish, and thirsty all the time. Will he be able to overcome his new diagnosis of Type 1 diabetes?

Olson, Michael and Olson, Steven. <u>How I Feel: A Book about Diabetes</u>. Lantern Books NY, 2004. (Grades 3-7)
- The authors show a little brother's experience with diabetes through words and pictures. Factual research is included.

Telgemeier, Raina and Martin, Ann Matthew (Creator). <u>Truth About Stacy</u> (Baby-Sitters Club Series #2). Scholastic, Inc., 2006. (Grades 4-7)
- Stacy not only has to deal with her diabetes diagnosis, her family just moved to a new town. Thankfully, she is able to make new friends who understand her disease.

Disability

Gleitzman, Morris. <u>Blabber Mouth</u>. Harcourt, 1995. (Grades 4-8)
- ~ Rowena Batts has an inborn disability that renders her incapable of speaking. She lives with her good-natured father. She was formerly enrolled in a special school where she grew adept at sign language, but now the girl and her father have moved to a new town, and she attends public school. There, her muteness and her comical surname make her an easy target for the class bully.

Klein, Robin. <u>Boss of the Pool</u>. Penguin USA, 1992. (Grades 5-8)
- ~ Shelley, who thinks the world should revolve around her, is upset when her mom takes a job at a home for mentally and physically handicapped children. In this story, Shelley teaches a boy with Downs Syndrome how to swim. Shelley finds herself, and is enlightened by what a great person her mom is. Shelley goes through a great change.

Sirof, Harriet. <u>Road Back</u>. iUniverse, Incorporated, 2000. (Grades 6-12)
- ~ The Road Back follows three teens who become disabled. It explores the obstacles they overcome to accept their disabilities and make new lives—covering hospitalization, rehabilitation, adjustments to school, friends and family, and problems of self-image and self-esteem.

Small, Mary. <u>Not Zackly</u>. Pascal Press, 1990. (Grades 5-8)
- ~ Deals with intellectual disability

Spence, Eleanor. <u>Nothing Place</u>. Harpercollins Juvenile Books, 1973. (Grades 9-12)

~ Learning to accept his partial deafness is bad enough, but having to adjust to a new neighborhood and a bunch of do-good friends is almost too much for Glen.

Vasil, Lisa. <u>Dark Secrets</u>. Collins Publishers Australia, 1989. (Grades 9-12)

~ Deals with blindness

Werlin, Nancy. <u>Are You Alone on Purpose?</u> Houghton Mifflin Company, 1994. (Grades 7-12)

~ Thirteen-year-old Alison Shandling has always been the good child: calming her autistic twin brother, deflecting her mother's rage, and pleasing her aloof father. Harry Roth has always been the cool kid who tests everyone's limits, especially those of his widowed father, the town's rabbi. The two dislike each other at first sight. When an accident confines Harry to a wheelchair, Alison   recognizes his frustration and loneliness and initiates a friendship.

Wrightson, Patricia. <u>I Own the Racecourse</u>. Hutchinson Radius, 1968. (Grades 6-12)

~ A mentally retarded boy thinks he has bought a race track for three dollars, and until a solution to the problem can be found, only the patience and understanding of his friends keep him from being hurt by the truth.

Divorce

Angell, Judie. <u>What's Best For You?</u> Bradbury, 1981. (Grades 7-9)
~ The complex and delicate relationships involving divorce are explained.

Arundel, Honor. <u>Family Failing, A</u>. Hamilton, 1972. (Grades 8-12)
~ After spending the summer in a commune, a teen-age girl feels better prepared to cope with the conflicts in her own family.

Baskin, Nora Raleigh. <u>Almost Home</u>. Scholastic. (Grades 5-10)
~ Leah hopes her new friend, Will, can help her through her parents' divorce.

Berger, Terry. <u>How Does it Feel When Your Parents Get Divorced?</u> Messner, 1977. (Grades 5-9)
~ The emotional problems experienced by children of divorce are discussed.

Blue, Rose. <u>Month of Sundays</u>. Franklin Watts, Incorporated, 1972. (Grades 5-8)
~ A ten-year old struggles to accept his parents' divorce and his new life in New York City.

Blume, Judy. <u>It's Not the End of the World</u>. Bradbury, 1972. (Grades 6-8)
~ This book discusses the confusion children experience during divorce.

Brashares, Ann. <u>Sisterhood of the Traveling Pants</u>. Dell Books for Young
  Readers, 2005. (Grades 7 and up)
  ~ The story of four very different friends who spend their summer
  apart. Each faces their own issues, but is comforted by the arrival
  of their thrift store jeans that magically fit everyone. Issues include
  having a friend with leukemia, relationship pressures, divorce, and
  family pressures.

Brooks, Bruce. <u>What Hearts</u>. HarperTeen, 1992. (Grades 5 and up)
  ~ It takes some time for Asa to accept first the divorce, then shortly
  thereafter, a new step-father, followed again by another divorce. He
  learns many valuable lessons.

Cohn, Rachel. <u>The Steps</u>. Simon & Schuster Children's Publishing, 2003.
  (Grades 6-8)
  ~ *The Steps* is a great realistic fiction about a girl named Annabel.
  She lives in New York City with her Mom and Grandma because her
  parents are divorced. Annabel learns that she has to go visit her Dad,
  who lives in Australia with his wife, Penney, and her disastrous kids,
  Lucy, Angus, and new baby Beatrice.

Dragonwagon, Crescent. <u>Always, Always</u>. Macmillan, 1984. (Grades 5
  and up)
  ~ A girl discovers that even though her parents are divorced, it doesn't
  change their love for her.

Ford, Melanie. <u>My Parents are Divorced Too: A Book for Kids by Kids</u>.
  Magination Books, 2006. (Grades 4-8)
  ~ Kids talk about their feelings associated with their parents' divorce.
  This book helps kids in similar situations understand that they're
  not alone.

Forrai, Maria. <u>A Look at Divorce</u>. Lerner, 1976. (Grades 4 and up)
  ~ Text and photographs describe problems faced by parents and
  children when a divorce occurs.

Gardner, Richard. <u>The Boys' and Girls' Book About Divorce</u>. Science
  House, 1970. (Grades 5-8)
  ~ Deals with childhood fears and worries common to children of
  divorce.

Klein, Norma. <u>Breaking Up</u>. Knopf Books for Young Readers, 1980.
  (Grades 9-12)
  ~ While she is visiting her father and stepmother in California,
  15-year-old Alison learns her mother is a lesbian.

Klein, Robin. <u>Hating Alison Ashley</u>. Viking Childrens Books, 1985.
(Grades 6-12)
~ Sixth-grader Erica Yurkin has always felt superior to everyone
in her school until redistricting brings beautiful, perfect and self-
assured Alison Ashley to the sixth grade. Erica hates her from the
very first. A series of events makes her realize that, although Alison
has material things, her mother is never there for her, while Erica has
the love and devotion of her family.

Leach, Norman. <u>My Wicked Step-Mother</u>.   Macmillan, 1993.
(Grades 4-8)
~ When his father remarries, Tom has a difficult time accepting his
new step-mother.

Mayle, Peter. <u>Why Are We Getting a Divorce</u>? Harmony, 1988. (All ages)
~ A handbook offering "reassurance, sympathy, and sound advice on
how to cope" for a family going through a divorce.

Nicholls, Bron. <u>Three Way Street</u>.   Random House Children's, 1983.
(Grades 5-12)
~ A realistic novel told by Aggie, twelve, who lives in Melbourne
with her mother, siblings and new dog, Bruce.

Prokop, Michael. <u>Divorce Happens to the Nicest Kids</u>. Alegra House,
1996. (Grades 3-8)
~ Helps kids understand divorce and alleviates some of their fears
associated with this issue.

Voigt, Cynthia. <u>Solitary Blue</u>. Aladdin Library, 2003. (Grades 7-12)
~ Jeff Greene was only seven when Melody, his mother, left him with
his reserved, undemonstrative father, the Professor. Years later, she
comes back and has Jeff spend the summer with her. During his
second summer with her, he is betrayed.

Drug Abuse

Anonymous. <u>Go Ask Alice</u>. Simon Pulse, 1998. (Grades 9 & up)
    ~ A true journal of one teen's highs and ultimate lows associated with drug abuse

Bell, Ruth. <u>Changing Bodies, Changing Lives: A Book for Teens on Sex and Relationships.</u> Vintage Books USA, 1988. (Grades 8 and up)
    ~ Addresses the need for open dialogue between teenagers on the topics of sex and relationships. Informs them on how to prevent unwanted pregnancies and sexually transmitted diseases. Updated to include material on suicide, AIDS and food and drug abuse.

Banks, Lynne. <u>Writing on the Wall</u>. Harpercollins Juvenile Books, 1982. (Grades 9-12)
    ~ A teenage girl takes a journey of self-discovery with her boyfriend, and unwittingly becomes involved in drug smuggling.

Carey, Gabrielle and Lette, Kathy. <u>Puberty Blues</u>. Pan Macmillan, 2002. (Grades 9-12)
    ~ Kathy Lette and Gabrielle Carey wrote this novel when they were eighteen. This is an account of growing up in the 1970s. Only the gang and the surf count. It's a hilarious and horrifying account of the way many teenagers live... and some of them die.

Childress, Alice. <u>Hero Ain't Nothin' but a Sandwich</u>. Sagebrush Education Resources, 1999. (Grades 7-12).
    ~ Presented in 23 short narratives, it is the story of an arrogant black teenager whose fragmented domestic life and addiction to heroin led him into delinquency.

Desetta, Al, M.A. and Wolin, Sybil, Ph.D. <u>The Struggle to Be Strong True Stories by Teens About Overcoming Tough Times.</u> Free Spirit Publishing. (Grades 7 and up)
~ In 30 first-person accounts, teens tell how they overcame major life obstacles, including, drug abuse by loved ones, interracial relationships, abandonment, homosexuality, and more.

Donaghy, Bronwyn. <u>Anna's Story.</u> HarperCollins, 1996. (Grades 7-12)
~ Anna's Story is a true tale of a fifteen-year-old popular girl, loved by everyone. However, her friends taught her that drugs and alcohol were the way of life - the only way to have a good time. One night Anna went too far at a party. The result was a not-so-happy ending.

Draper, Sharon. <u>Forged By Fire</u>. Simon Pulse, 1998. (Grades 6-12)
~ This prequel to Draper's Tears of a Tiger is a stark portrayal of a young man struggling to protect his little sister from a drug-addicted mother and an abusive father.

Klein, Robin. <u>Came Back to Show You I Could Fly</u>. Penguin USA, 1990. (Grades 8-12)
~ *Came Back To Show You I Could Fly* is about an eleven year old boy named Seymour who meets Angie, an older adventurous drug addict, but Seymour does not know this. She is in a great deal of debt to drug dealers and has been dis-owned by her family. Seymour too, is having family problems

Lipsyte, Robert. <u>The Contender</u>. HarperTrophy, 1987. (Grades 6-9)
~ Alfred is a high-school dropout working at a grocery store. His best friend is in a haze of drugs and violence, and now some street punks are harassing him for something he didn't do. Alfred gathers up the courage to visit Donatelli's Gym, the neighborhood's boxing club. He wants to be a champion--on the streets and in his own life.

Packer, Alex J., Ph.D. <u>HIGHS! Over 150 Ways to Feel Really, REALLY Good…Without Alcohol or Other Drugs.</u> Free Spirit Publishing. (Grades 7 and up)
~ Packer outlines natural highs, such as: breathing and meditation, sports and exercise, food, the senses, nature, creativity, family, friends, and more.

Ponton, Lynn, MD. <u>The Sex Lives of Teenagers: Revealing the Secret World of Adolescent Boys and Girls</u>. Plume Books, 2001. (Grades 9 and up)

- With more and more teenagers having sex by the age of sixteen and others feeling pressured to before they're ready, parents and adolescents must find ways to communicate openly and honestly about a subject that has been ignored for too long. Lynn Ponton, M.D., takes a look at what teenagers have to say about their sexual lives. In a safe forum, without fear of judgment or censorship, teens feel free to speak frankly about their feelings, desires, fantasies, and expectations. And parents give voice to the struggle of coming to terms with their children's emerging sexual identities.   Dr. Ponton opens a dialogue that addresses controversial topics such as pregnancy, abortion, masturbation, sexual orientation, Internet dating, and gender roles. Sensitive subjects such as AIDS and drugs are also explored.

Rebman, Renee. <u>Addictions and Risky Behaviors: Cutting, Bingeing, Snorting, and Other Risky Behaviors</u>. Enslow Publishers, Incorporated, 2006.
-The causes and signs of these addictions are addressed by Rebman. Also addressed is how those who are addicted can be helped.

Scott, Sharon. <u>How to Say No and Keep Your Friends: Peer Pressure Reversal for Teens and Preteens</u>. Human Resource Development Press, 1997. (Grades 5-12)
- This book presents teens/preteens with very specific ways to manage all kinds of negative peer pressure--from gossip and cliques to the most serious problem invitations including drugs, sex, and even violence.

Stewart, Bridgett, and White, Franklin. <u>No Matter What</u>. Blue/Black Press, 2002. (Grades 7-12)
- Bridgett Stewart shares her journey through unthinkable poverty and discusses everything from gaining her own self-respect when no one else would respect her because of where she lived to surviving verbal abuse from classmates, living without a father, school pressures, and her decision to use education as a vehicle from poverty while earning a 4.0 grade point average in tough and trying times. Stewart also discusses self-esteem, alcohol and drugs, and many other topics.

Eating Disorders – Anorexia And Bulimia

Berg, Francis. <u>Children & Teens Afraid to Eat</u>. Healthy Weight Publishing Network, 2000. (Grades 6 and up)
⁓ This book focuses on the most pathological problems: anorexia and bulimia nervosa and binge eating. This is primarily a how-to-cope guide for family members of the afflicted.

Cherin, Kim. <u>The Hungry Self</u>. Perennial, 1994. (Grades 9-12)
⁓ Some five million American women suffer from eating disorders ranging from compulsive dieting to compulsive eating, anorexia, and bulimia. *The Hungry Self* explores the often troubled relationship between mothers and daughters and how daughters of all ages and backgrounds often flee the struggle for identity and self-development into an obsession with food.

Claude-Pierre, Peggy. <u>The Secret Language of Eating Disorders</u>. Vintage Books USA, 1999. (Grades 10 and up)
⁓ The book describes the five stages of recovery, discusses the challenges of working with them at home, and presents a plan for working with health professionals.

Hall, Alissa. <u>The Thinnest Girl Alive: Diary of a Young Dancer</u>. Raven's Perch Books, 2006. (Grades 7 and up)
⁓ Told in the form of a diary, Hall takes the reader through a young girl's viewpoint.

Hall, Cohn, and Cohen. <u>Bulimia: A Guide to Recovery</u>. Gurze Books, 1999. (Grades 9 and up)
    ~ This book includes answers to questions most often asked about bulimia, insight from more than 400 recovered and recovering bulimics, a three-week program to stop bingeing, specific advice for loved-ones, things to do instead of bingeing, Lindsey Hall's own inspiring story, "Eat Without Fear," and suggestions from professional eating disorders therapists.

Hautzig, Deborah. <u>Second Star to the Right</u>. Puffin Books, 1999. (Grades 9-12)
    ~ Leslie Hiller is a bright, attractive, talented teenager who leads a privileged life in New York City. She is also a perfectionist. When Leslie starts to diet, she finds herself becoming obsessed, getting thinner and thinner, until she is forced to realize that her quest for perfection is killing her.

Hornbacher, Marya. <u>Wasted : A Memoir of Anorexia and Bulimia</u>. Perennial, 1999. (Grades 7-12)
    ~ Hornbacher sustains both anorexia and bulimia through five lengthy hospitalizations, endless therapy, and the loss of family, friends, jobs, and ultimately, any sense of what it means to be "normal." By the time she is in college, Hornbacher is in the grip of a bout with anorexia so horrifying that it will forever put to rest the romance of wasting away.

Lipton, Leslie. <u>Unwell: a Novel</u>. Iuniverse, Inc., 2006. (Grades 7-12)
    ~ A first-hand account of anorexia. This book gives readers a view of this Disease from the inside out.

Medoff, Jillian. <u>Hunger Point</u>. ReganBooks, 2002. (Grades 10 and up)
    ~ This novel attempts to unravel the familial and social pressures that drive twosisters into a life of serious food abuse. One survives, the other doesn't. Frannie, though she does not succumb completely to anorexia, is near the breaking point, and *Hunger Point* takes us along on her painful and often funny emotional odyssey of rebirth, detailed with her family's love and her own self-loathing.

Menzie, Morgan. <u>Diary of an Anorexic Girl</u>. W Publishing Group, 2003. (Grades 7-12)
    ~ Morgan Menzie takes readers through a harrowing but ultimately hopeful and inspiring account of her eating disorder. Her story is told through the journals she kept during her daily struggle with this addiction and disease.

Morall, Heather. <u>The Echo Glass: A Novel about Anorexia Nervosa</u>. Rubery Press, 2006. (Grades 8 and up)
Jasmine escapes bullying by obsessing over her own weight. This eventually leads to an even tougher struggle – anorexia.

Rees, Elizabeth. <u>Body Lines</u>. Simon Pulse; Aladdin Paperbacks, 1998. (Grades 7 and up)
~ Daly goes on a dangerous diet when her dance school is jeopardized.

Sacker. <u>Dying to Be Thin</u>. Warner Books, 1987. (Grades 9 and up)
~ Packed with information on how, when and where anorexics, bulimics, and their families can seek help, this book provides a caring comprehensive examination of anorexia and bulimia.

Sparks, Beatrice. <u>Kim: Empty Inside: The Diary of an Anonymous Teenager</u>. Avon Books, 2002. (Grades 7-10)
~ Seventeen-year-old Kim, feeling the pressure of maintaining an A average to stay on her college gymnastics team, becomes obsessive about her weight and develops anorexia.

Eating Disorders – Obesity

Bell, Ruth. <u>Changing Bodies, Changing Lives: A Book for Teens on Sex and Relationships.</u> Vintage Books USA, 1988. (Grades 8 and up)
‐ Addresses the need for open dialogue between teenagers on the topics of sex and relationships. Informs them on how to prevent unwanted pregnancies and sexually transmitted diseases. Updated to include material on suicide, AIDS and food and drug abuse. Berg, Francis.

<u>Children & Teens Afraid to Eat</u>. Healthy Weight Publishing Network, 2000. (Grades 6 and up)
‐ This book focuses on the most pathological problems: anorexia and bulimia nervosa and binge eating. This is primarily a how-to-cope guide for family members of the afflicted.

Cherin, Kim. <u>The Obsession</u>. Perennial, 1994. (Grades 9-12)
‐ *The Obsession* is an analysis of our society's increasing demand that women be thin. It offers a careful, thought provoking discussion of the reasons men have encouraged this obsession and women have embraced it. It is a book about women's efforts to become thin rather than to accept the natural dimensions of their bodies--a book about the meaning of food and its rejection.

Fowler, Thurley. <u>Hippo Doing the Backstroke</u>. Hodder Headline Australia, 1989. (Grades 5-10)
‐ Greg Anderson is a boy who enjoys eating, but both his figure and his swimming style suffer as a result. However, his grandmother's

program of exercise, hard work and diet help Greg overcome his weight problems.

Lynn, Bunkie. <u>The Big Girls' Guide to Life: A Plus-Sized Jaunt Through a Body-Obsessed World</u>. Ladybug Pub Llc, 2003. (Grades 9 and up)
   ~ *The Big Girls' Guide to Life* celebrates "Life as a Big Girl with Attitude!"

Shanker, Wendy. <u>Fat Girl's Guide to Life</u>. Bloomsbury Publishing PLC, 2004. (Grades 10 and up)
   ~ Wendy explores dieting issues, full-figured fashions, and feminist philosophy while guiding you through exercise clubs, doctor's offices, shopping malls, and even the bedroom. She believes that you can be fit and fat, even as the weight loss industry conspires to make you think otherwise. *The Fat Girl's Guide to Life* invites you to step off the scale and weigh the issues for yourself.

Wilensky, Amy. <u>The Weight of It: A Story of Two Sisters</u>. Henry Holt & Company, 2004. (Grades 9-12)
   ~ As young girls, a year apart in age, Alison and Amy Wilensky were almost indistinguishable. And they were inseparable: growing up in a comfortable Boston suburb, they were never far from each other's side, wearing matching dresses, playing the same games, eating the same food. But Alison began gaining weight in elementary school and by the time she was sixteen was morbidly obese. The sisters remained close, but over the years the daily ridicule and insecurity endured by Alison took their toll, reshaping her identity and affecting the sisters' relationship in unanticipated ways.

Food Allergies

Ballard, Carol. Special Diets and Food Allergies. Heinemann, 2006. (Grades 6 and up)

- Ballard answers questions about lactose intolerance, diet and diabetes, weight, food intolerance, and more. This book also explains how some people's bodies react to certain foods and how to manage that.

Glaser, Jason and Hubbard, Jason R. Food Allergies. Coughlan Publishing, 2006. (Grades 4 and up)

- Addresses questions kids have about their allergies, and provides resources to help kids deal with their allergies.

Gordon, Sherri Mabry. Peanut Butter, Milk, and Other Deadly Threats: What You Should Know about Food Allergies. Enslow Publishers, Incorporated, 2006. (Grades 5-9)

- Discusses what food allergies are, how to be tested for them, how a body responds during a reaction, and treatments. This book includes suggestions for how to live safely without giving up social experiences.

Powell, Jillian and Lousie, John (Ed.). Aneil Has a Food Allergy. Chelsea House Publishers, 2004. (Grades 2-4)

Schrand, Tracy. A Day at the Playground: A Food Allergy Awareness for the Young. Llumina Press, 2006. (Grades 2-4)

- Targets young children with tips on how to have fun, but be safe with food allergies.

Vanderwoude, Jennifer.   <u>Learning Experience: A Story for Teens with Anaphylaxis</u>. iUniverse, Incorporated, 2007. (Grades 8-12)
- Kaylee is starting her first year of high school. Thus far, she's dealt with her peanut allergy just fine. Now, she's feeling more pressure to fit in. Will her food allergy get in the way of her life?

Weiner, Ellen and Gosselin, Kim (Ed.). <u>Taking Food Allergies to School</u>. JayJo Books, Llc, 1999. (Grades K-4)
- Written for kids, but also helpful for those adults in their life, topics include sharing lunches, special parties and snacks for the entire class. Also included is a quiz for kids to help them understand the dangers of food allergies, and "Ten Tips for Teachers to Consider" when working with a child who has food allergies.

Foster Care

Ballard, Kimberly M. <u>Light at Summer's End</u>. WaterBrook Press, 1994.
(Grades 8 and up)
- Dumped off at a lady's house for the summer, fourteen-year-old Melissa and her new guardian develop a friendship as they work through the hurts of the past and grapple with the issue of abortion.

Burch, Jennings Michael. <u>They Cage the Animals at Night</u>. Signet, 1988.
- Burch was left at an orphanage and never stayed at any one foster home long enough to make any friends. This is the story of how he grew up and gained the courage to reach out for love.

Byars, Betsy. <u>Pinballs</u>. HarperTrophy, 1992. (Grades 4-8)
- Carlie knows she's got no say in what happens to her. Stuck in a foster home with two other kids, Harvey and Thomas J, she's just a pinball being bounced from bumper to bumper. As soon as you get settled, somebody puts another coin in the machine and off you go again. But against her will and her better judgment, Carlie and the boys become friends. And all three of them start to see that they can take control of their own lives.

Cresswell, Helen. <u>Dear Shrink</u>. Ulverscroft Large Print Books, 1987.
(Grades 5-12)
- When the woman looking after them in their parents' absence dies suddenly, three children find themselves in foster care and must use all their courage and ingenuity to cope with the situation.

Hahn, Mary Downing. <u>Daphne's Book</u>. Clarion, 1983. (Grades 6-12)

~ Daphne and her sister live with their grandma because their parents have died. However, their grandma is emotionally troubled, and both girls are placed in an institutional setting; eventually, they are placed with a cousin.

Holz, Loretta. Foster Child. Messner, 1981. (Grades 5-8)
~ After Peter's dad leaves and his mother begins drinking heavily, he is placed in foster care.

Nixon, Joan Lowry. Caught in the Act. Bantam, 1988. (Grades 6-12)
~ Mike was adopted by German immigrants, mistreated, and placed with a new family.

Rowlands, Avril. Letty. London: Puffin, 1984. (Grades 5-8)
~ Unwanted by her parents, Letty has spent most of her life in a children's home. She often gets in trouble and hopes for a home with a family.

Spence, Eleanor. The Left Overs. Routledge, 1982. (Grades 9-12)
~ When the home in which they've been living is about to be closed down to make way for a new road, four foster children write an advertisement for a real home with a proper family.

Warner, Sally. This Isn't About the Money. Viking Books, 2002. (Grades 5-8)
~ 12 year old Janey and her sister become orphans when the car they're riding in is hit by a drunk driver. She struggles to keep her parents' spirit alive by trying to convince her new guardians (her grandpa and great aunt), that her parents' memories are worth more than the lawsuit. Eventually, Janey and her sister find a new kind of love from their foster parents.

Friendship

Booher, Dianna. <u>Boyfriends and Boy Friends</u>. Baker Pub Group, 1988.
(Grades 6 and up)
- Despite the insistence of everyone around her that boys and girls cannot be ordinary friends, teenaged Leanne is determined to maintain her long-standing, non-romantic, friendship with the troubled Jared.

Brashares, Ann. <u>Sisterhood of the Traveling Pants</u>. Dell Books for Young Readers, 2005. (Grades 7 and up)
- The story of four very different friends who spend their summer apart. Each faces their own issues, but is comforted by the arrival of their thrift store jeans that magically fit everyone. Issues include having a friend with leukemia, relationship pressures, divorce, and family pressures.

Brashares, Ann. <u>Second Summer of the Sisterhood</u>. Dell Books for Young Readers, 2006. (Grades 8 and up)
- Another summer is spent apart for the 4 friends. Again, each is comforted by the pair of thrift store jeans when they face issues such as: love lost and found, death, and finding the courage to live honestly.

Brashares, Ann. <u>Girls in Pants: The Third Summer of the Sisterhood</u>. Dell Books for Young Readers, 2007. (Grades 7 and up)
- The third summer begins after the girls' high school graduation. The girls keep their ties close as they again face new issues. This time they face budding relationships, new step-siblings, tragedy in the family, and more heartbreak.

Brashares, Ann. <u>Forever in Blue: The Fourth Summer of the Sisterhood</u>. Delacorte Books for Young Readers, 2007. (Grades 8 and up)
~ This book takes a look at the girls' first take on college/post-high school life. Along with new opportunities come new issues: new love interests, loss of virginity, and breakups and make-ups.

Cabot, Meg. <u>How to be Popular.</u> Harper Teen, 2008 (Grades 8-12)
~ Steph is obsessing over becoming popular and is using an old book entitled "How to Be Popular" to help her. The question is, will she realize what's really important in her life or not?

Clifton, Lucille. <u>My Friend Jacob</u>. Dutton, 1980. (Grades 4-8)
~ A young boy tells about Jacob, who though older and mentally challenged, is his best friend.

Crutcher, Chris. <u>Staying Fat for Sarah Byrnes</u>. HarperCollins Publishers, 2003. (Grades 7 and up)
~ The daily class discussions about the nature of man, the existence of God, abortion, organized religion, suicide and other contemporary issues serve as a backdrop for a high-school senior's attempt to answer a friend's dramatic cry for help.

Courtney, Vicky. Teenvirtue: <u>Real Issues, Real Life. . . A Teen Girl's Survival Guide</u>. B&H Publishing Group, 2005. (Grades 6-12)
~ Offers Christian advice for issues such as: friendships, boys, fashion and beauty, and heavier issues such as Internet safety, sex and drugs. The format is not "preachy," but resembles that of popular magazines.

Courtney, Vicki. <u>Teenvirtue 2: A Teen Girl's Guide to Relationships</u>. B&H Publishing Group, 2006. (Grades 6-12)
~ Includes Christian advice for relationships including with friends, with boys, and with God.

Dessen, Sarah. <u>Keeping the Moon</u>. Penguin USA, 2004. (Grades 6 and up)
~ Fifteen-year-old Colie has never fit in. First, it was because she was fat. Then, after she lost the weight, it was because of a reputation that she didn't deserve. So when she's sent to stay with her eccentric aunt Mira for the summer, Colie doesn't expect too much. After all, why would anyone in Colby, North Carolina, want to bother with her when no one back home does?

Feuer, Elizabeth. <u>One Friend to Anot</u>. Simon Pulse, 1988. (Grades 7 and up)

~ A painfully real story of a seventh grader who wants to change her image, and faces public humiliation at the hands of a new "friend."

Hutson, Joan. We're Friends Because. Pauline Books & Media, 1995. (Grades 4-8)
~ Reflections on such aspects of friendship as sharing and forgiveness.

Marsden, John. Take My Word For It. Pan Publishing, 1993. (Grades 9-12)
~ While writing in a journal for class, Lisa gradually reveals her own personal feelings and concerns, while describing relationships with and problems of other girls at her boarding school.

O'Roark Dowell, Francis. The Secret Language of Girls. Aladdin, 2005. (Grades 4-8)
~ Deals with two friends' transitions to middle school as they choose different   interests and end up at different tables. Addresses many issues associated with middle school.

Packer, Alex J., Ph.D. The How Rude!™ Handbook of Friendship & Dating Manners for Teens Surviving the Social Scene. Free Spirit Publishing. (Grades 7 and up)
~ Young adults learn how to have successful relationships.

Philbrick, Rodman R. and Philbrick, W.R. Freak the Mighty. Scholastic, Inc., 2001. (Grades 6-10)
~ At the beginning of eighth grade, learning disabled Max and his new friend Freak, whose birth defect has affected his body but not his brilliant mind, find that when they combine forces they make a powerful team.

Rainey, Dennis, Barbara, Samuel, and Rebecca. So You're About to Be a Teenager: Godly Advice for Preteens on Friends, Love, Sex, Faith and Other Life Issues. Nelson Books, 2003. (Grades 6 and up)
~ Samuel and Rebecca Rainey share their perspective as young adults who recall their own successes and failures as teenagers. They cover the topics of friends, peer pressure, boundaries, dating, and sex. The Raineys address the most common traps of adolescence and teach young people how to avoid making poor choices.

Randle, Kristen D. The Only Alien on the Planet. Scholastic, 1996. (Grades 7 and up)
~ Ginny Christianson had been a happy person. When her family suddenly relocates and a beloved older brother leaves for college at

the same time, Ginny is a "displaced person." As life manages to go on, and fun, caring new friends begin to fill the gap, a strange boy at school captures Ginny's attention. Smitty Tibbs is a brilliant, handsome boy who never speaks. He is known as the Alien and lives in total isolation from emotion and communication--tolerated by the other students but pretty much left alone. (*Anne O'Malley*)

Saul, Laya. <u>You Don't Have to Learn Everything the Hard Way: What I Wish Someone Had Told Me</u>. Kadima Press, 2004. (Grades 8 and up)
~ Reading this book first can help young adults avoid dangerous situations and possible regrets later on. Ms. Saul shares her life lessons with young adults, including the following topics: Defining Boundaries, Gaining a New Perspective, Expecting the Unexpected, Choices that Change Your Life, Dealing with Failure and Regret, Pain and Suffering as Part of Living, Alcohol and Drug Abuse, Preventing Abuse, Life and Death, You and the World, Relationships, Family and Friends, Forgiveness, and Live Your Dreams.

Strasser, Todd. <u>Friends Till the End</u>. Laurel Leaf Books, 1981. (Grades 6-12)
~ David befriended a nerd and has to deal with peer pressure as he supports his new friend throughout his agonizing struggle with leukemia.

Werlin, Nancy. <u>Are You Alone on Purpose?</u> Houghton Mifflin Company, 1994. (Grades 7-12)
~ Thirteen-year-old Alison Shandling has always been the good child: calming her autistic twin brother, deflecting her mother's rage, and pleasing her aloof father. Harry Roth has always been the cool kid who tests everyone's limits, especially those of his widowed father, the town's rabbi. The two dislike each other at first sight. When an accident confines Harry to a wheelchair, Alison recognizes his frustration and loneliness and initiates a friendship.

Wild, Margaret. <u>Jinx</u>. Simon Pulse, 2004. (Grades 9 and up)
~ When Jen's boyfriend commits suicide, she is lonely, sad, bewildered, and rebellious. During this bleak period, she starts drinking and having casual sex, but then meets Ben and begins the long journey back to normalcy. After he dies, a classmate calls her "Jinx," and Jen decides the name fits her. Seeking to strike out at Hal, the person responsible for Ben's accident, and not realizing or caring where her angry words fall, Jinx conducts a secret, malicious assault. It is not

until she actually meets and becomes friends with Hal that she is able to begin putting aside the hurt and anger that have plagued her since childhood. In confronting and dealing with the family issues that have been a lingering shadow all her life, the teen learns that love and forgiveness are a first step to maturity. (*Sharon Morrison*)

Woodson, Jacqueline. I Hadn't Meant to Tell You This. Laurel-Leaf, 1995. (Grades 7 and up)

 ~ Two girls: one white, one black; one abused, one protected, both missing their mothers. An unlikely friendship ignites between the two, and, in sharing their differences, both of their lives are transformed.

Gender Issues

Abrahams, George and Ahlbrand, Sheila. <u>Boy V. Girl? How Gender Shapes Who We Are, What We Want, and How We Get Along.</u> Free Spirit Publishing. (Grades 7 And up)
    - Addresses several gender issues including gender roles and stereotypes, as well as how to deal with and overcome these in every day life.

Courtney, Vicky. <u>Teenvirtue: Real Issues, Real Life. . . A Teen Girl's Survival Guide.</u> B&H Publishing Group, 2005. (Grades 6-12)
    - Offers Christian advice for issues such as: friendships, boys, fashion and beauty, and heavier issues such as Internet safety, sex and drugs. The format is not "preachy," but resembles that of popular magazines.

Greenburg, Judith. <u>Girl's Guide to Growing Up: Making the Right Choices.</u> Scholastic Library Publishing, 2000. (Grades 5-8)
    - Addresses common issues faced in middle school, such as: relationships, temptations, self-image, risky behavior, and decisions middle school girls will be faced with.

Lantz, Francess. <u>The Day Joanie Frankenhauser Became a Boy.</u> Dutton Juvenile, 2004. (Grades 4-6)
    - A simple name misprint has Joanie pretending to be a "John." Gender lines are examined.

Muharrar, Aisha. <u>More Than a Label Why What You Wear or Who You're With Doesn't Define Who You Are.</u> Free Spirit Publishing. (Grades 6 – 12)

~ Written from the viewpoint of the 17-year-old author, various labels and how to deal with them are discussed. Also addressed are cliques, peer pressure, popularity, racism, sexism, and homophobia. This book empowers students and shows them how to assert their self-worth.

Schwager, Tina, P.T.A., A.T.C. and Schuerger, Michele. Gutsy Girls Young Women Who Dare. Free Spirit Publishing. (Grades 6 and up)
~ Tales of women succeeding in roles stereotypically male-driven

Ure, Jean. What If They Saw Me Now? New York: Delacorte Press, 1982. (Grades 9-12)
~ Jamie, a sixteen year old baseball star, faces peer ridicule when he discovers his unbelievable talent for ballet.

Gifted Students

Cormier, Robert. <u>The Chocolate War</u>. Laurel Leaf Books, 1974. (Grades 6-10)
- Jerry, a bright student, becomes a hero by refusing to sell chocolates. The author deals with peer pressure in high school, and teaches the reader that remaining true to one's beliefs may result in painful loneliness.

Delisle, Jim, Ph.D. and Galbraith, Judy, M.A. <u>When Gifted Kids Don't Have All the Answers: How to Meet Their Social and Emotional Needs</u>. Free Spirit Publishing. (Grades 6-12).
- This book offers proven, practical suggestions for encouraging social and emotional growth among gifted, talented, and creative children and youth. Through this book, a child's personal needs are addressed.

Elkind, David. <u>All Grown Up and No Place to Go: Teenagers in Crisis</u>. Perseus Books Group, 1997. (Grades 9 and up)
- Elkind makes a case for protecting teens instead of pressuring them. This book addresses long work hours, rising violence, and pregnancies.

Galbraith, Judy, M.A., and Delisle, Jim, Ph.D. <u>The Gifted Kids' Survival Guide: A Teen Handbook</u>. Free Spirit Publishing. (Grades 7 and up).
- Through this book, teens learn more about their giftedness, testing, and how to manage their stress.

Greenspon, Thomas S., Ph.D. <u>Freeing Our Families from Perfectionism</u>. Free Spirit Publishing. (Grades 9 and up)

~ Tom Greenspon explains perfectionism, where it comes from, and what to do about it. Readers will learn how to change perfectionism into self-acceptance.

Kelleher, Victor. <u>Del-Del</u>. Random House, 1993. (Grades 9-12)
~ A teenage girl in Sydney, Australia, records how her family is devastated by her older sister's death and by the bizarre behavior of her gifted younger brother, who seems to be cold and unfeeling.

McCutcheon, Randall. <u>Get Off My Brain A Survival Guide for Lazy*</u> <u>Students (*Bored, Frustrated, and Otherwise Sick of School).</u> Free Spirit Publishing.
(Grades 6 and up)
~ The author, who is also a teacher and knows how irrelevant school can seem to   gifted students, suggests creative, fun, and effective strategies for succeeding in school.

Paulsen, Gary. <u>The Island</u>. Franklin Watts, Inc., 1981. (Grades 9-12)
~ Through Will Neuton, the reader learns that gifted young men need to pass through the stages of adolescence and early manhood at a different pace and in a different way.

Roehlkepartain, Jolene. <u>Surviving School Stress</u>. Group Pub Inc., 1990. (Grades 6-12)
~ Focuses on school-related stress and how to deal with it from a Christian perspective. Discusses grades, parents' expectations, after-school activities, and getting along with people who have different beliefs.

Selzer, Adam. <u>How to Get Suspended and Influence People</u>. Random House Children's Books, 2007. (Grades 6 and up)
~ As an assignment for his gifted and talented class, Leon decides to "educate sixth and seventh graders" with a video on sex education. He started out in his smart-aleck, humorous ways, but began seeing his video as truly educational and comforting to those going through puberty. Soon, the whole town is in on this issue, as his video is censored out and he is suspended.

Sparks, Beatrice. <u>Kim: Empty Inside: The Diary of an Anonymous Teenager</u>. Avon Books, 2002. (Grades 7-10)
~ Seventeen-year-old Kim, feeling the pressure of maintaining an A average to stay on her college gymnastics team, becomes obsessive about her weight and develops anorexia.

Yee, Lisa. <u>Millicent Min, Girl Genius</u>. Arthur A. Levine, 2003. (Grades 5-8)

    - *Millicent Min* is about a 12 year old girl in the 11th grade. She is really smart and wants to spend her summer reading and taking a college class. Her mom signs her up for volleyball and she's not accepted by the other kids. In order to keep a new friend, she lies about her intelligence and all of her accomplishments.

Zindel, Paul. <u>The Amazing and Death-Defying Diary of Eugene Dingman</u>. Bantam, 1987. (Grades 9-12)

    - Through a diary, Eugene discovers several truths about himself.

Zindel, Paul. <u>Confessions of a Teenage Baboon</u>. Bantam Books, 1987. (Grades 9-12).

    - Chris helps the readers understand that reaching adulthood may be a long, hard journey filled with traumatic experiences which can help them become better individuals.

Growing Up And Maturation

Angelou, Maya. <u>I Know Why the Caged Bird Sings</u>. Bantam Books, 1983. (Grades 8-12)
    - Poet Maya Angelou recounts a youth filled with disappointment, frustration, tragedy, and finally hard-won independence. Sent at a young age to live with her grandmother in Arkansas, Angelou learned a great deal from this exceptional woman and the tightly knit black community there. These very lessons carried her throughout the hardships she endured later in life, including a tragic occurrence while visiting her mother in St. Louis and her formative years spent in California--where an unwanted pregnancy changed her life forever.

Baker, Russell. <u>Growing Up</u>. Plume Books, 1995. (Grades 9 and up)
    - This is an autobiographical story of growing up in America between the world wars. It is the story of adversity and courage, of love and the awkwardness of sex, of family bonds and family tensions.

Baldwin, James. <u>Go Tell It on the Mountain</u>. Laurel, 1985. (Grades 6 and up)
    - Baldwin chronicles a fourteen-year-old boy's discovery of the terms of his identity as the stepson of the minister of a storefront Pentecostal church in Harlem one Saturday in March of 1935. Baldwin explores spirituality, sexuality, and moral struggles of self-invention.

Bronte, Charlotte. <u>Jane Eyre</u>. Signet Book, 1997. (Grades 9 and up)
    - The story of an unhappy orphan and her life as a governess at Thornfield is filled with difficulty, including a shocking revelation

on her wedding day. The happy ending finally arrives, though, and Jane and Rochester are united forever.

Buckman, Michelle. <u>Maggie Come Lately</u>. NavPublishing Group, 2007. (Grades 7 and up)

    - At age 4, Maggie witnessed her mother's suicide. Since then, Maggie has been the parent, housekeeper, and the responsible person in the house since her dad has abandoned his responsibilities, including her two younger brothers. At age 16, Maggie has found a new identity as a popular person, and is struggling with who she really is and what her values are. She really comes into her own after a sexual assault.

Carlson, Melody. <u>Becoming Me: Diary of a Teenage Girl, Book 1</u>. Multnomah, 2000. (Grades 8-10)

    - The story of a Christian girl's transition from childhood to womanhood. Issues addressed include: peer pressure, loyalty, conflict with parents, the longing for a boyfriend, and her own spirituality.

Conroy, Frank. <u>Stop-Time</u>. Penguin Books, 1993. (Grades 9-12)

    - This is an autobiography that is a memoir of boyhood and adolescence. Beginning with a lesson in brutality at a progressive boarding school, the book moves to a self-help settlement in Florida, a Connecticut mental hospital (where Conroy's mother and stepfather are wardens), and to New York City (where he survives by his wits in schools, at jobs, and even more dangerously at home). Then, after his mother leaves for Europe and his stepfather installs an insane mistress in the family's apartment, Conroy runs away, embarking on new adventures.

Creech, Sharon. <u>Bloomability</u>. HarperTrophy, 1999. (Grades 5-8)

    - Dinnie grows up during a forced trip to Switzerland as she attends her uncle's school.

Creech, Sharon. <u>Chasing Redbird</u>. HarperTrophy, 1998. (Grades 5-8)

    - Zinnia, as the quiet, middle feels invisible until she works to uncover a mysterious path. Along the way, she learns about her family's history and creates her own path to adulthood.

Creech, Sharon. <u>Ruby Holler</u>. HarperTrophy, 2004. (Grades 5-8)

    - Dallas and Florida are orphans who appear hopeless and rebellious. Tiller and Sairy are an older couple who invite the twins to join them on their journeys. Through the magic of Ruby Holler they all grow closer and grow up.

Courtney, Vicky. <u>Teenvirtue: Real Issues, Real Life. . . A Teen Girl's Survival Guide</u>. B&H Publishing Group, 2005. (Grades 6-12)
- Offers Christian advice for issues such as: friendships, boys, fashion and beauty, and heavier issues such as Internet safety, sex and drugs. The format is not "preachy," but resembles that of popular magazines.

Dickens, Charles. <u>Great Expectations</u>. Penguin Books, 2003. (Grades 10 and up)
- This novel contains many themes and issues. A virtual encyclopedia of human emotions--fear, child abuse, anticipation, disappointment, love, jealousy, manipulation--this greatest of all of Dickens' novels has everything. Pip is a character who is aware of his feelings and, still, because he is human, he allows these emotions to sometimes compel him to do the opposite of what is right and best.

Frank, Anne. <u>The Diary of a Young Girl</u>. Bantam Books, 1993. (Grades 7-10)
- Anne Frank received a blank diary on her 13th birthday, just weeks before she and her family went into hiding in Nazi-occupied Amsterdam. Her detailed, personal entries chronicle 25 trying months of claustrophobic, quarrelsome intimacy with her parents, sister, a second family, and a middle-aged dentist who has little tolerance for Anne's vivacity.

Golding, William. <u>Lord of the Flies</u>. Perigee, 1959. (Grades 8-12)
- This is a classic tale about a group of English schoolboys who are plane-wrecked on a deserted. At first, the stranded boys cooperate, attempting to gather food, make shelters, and maintain signal fires. Overseeing their efforts are Ralph, "the boy with fair hair," and Piggy. Although Ralph tries to impose order and delegate responsibility, there are many in their number who would rather swim, play, or hunt the island's wild pig population. The situation deteriorates as the trappings of civilization continue to fall away, until Ralph discovers that instead of being hunters, he and Piggy have become the hunted.

Greenburg, Judith. <u>Girl's Guide to Growing Up: Making the Right Choices</u>. Scholastic Library Publishing, 2000. (Grades 5-8)
- Addresses common issues faced in middle school, such as: relationships, temptations, self-image, risky behavior, and decisions middle school girls will be faced with.

Greene, Bette. <u>The Summer of My German Soldier</u>. Penguin, 1999. (Grades 7-12)
~ When German prisoners of war are brought to her Arkansas town during World War II, twelve-year-old Patty, a Jewish girl, befriends one of them and must deal with the consequences of that friendship.

Hemingway, Ernest. <u>The Nick Adams Stories</u>. Scribner Book Company, 1981. (Grades 9-12)
~ The famous "Nick Adams" stories show a memorable character growing from child to adolescent to soldier, veteran, writer, and parent -- a sequence closely paralleling the events of Hemingway's life.

Hinton, S.E. <u>The Outsiders</u>. Prentice Hall, 1997. (Grades 7-12)
~ According to Ponyboy, there are two kinds of people in the world: one has money, can get away with just about anything, and the other always lives on the outside and needs to watch his back. Ponyboy learns how to live as a greaser in a family whose parents have passed away.

Hughes, Langston. <u>Not Without Laughter</u>. Touchstone Books, 1995. (Grades 8-12)
~ Depicts a Black family's attempts to deal with life in a small Kansas town.

Klein, Robin. <u>Boss of the Pool</u>. Penguin USA, 1992. (Grades 5-8)
~ Shelley, who thinks the world should revolve around her, is upset when her mom takes a job at a home for mentally and physically handicapped children. In this story, Shelley teaches a boy with Downs Syndrome how to swim. Shelley finds herself, and is enlightened by what a great person her mom is. Shelley goes through a great change.

Knowles, John. <u>A Separate Peace</u>. Scribner Book Company, 2003. (Grades 9-12)
~ Set at a boys' boarding school in New England during the early years of World War II, *A Separate Peace* is a story about the dark side of adolescence. Gene is a lonely, introverted intellectual. Phineas is a handsome, taunting, daredevil athlete. What happens between the two friends one summer, like the war itself, banishes the innocence of these boys and their world.

Lee, Harper. <u>To Kill a Mockingbird</u>. Little Brown & Company, 1988. (Grades 8-12)

⁓ A lawyer's advice to his children as he defends the real mockingbird of Harper Lee's classic novel--a black man charged with the rape of a white girl. Through the young eyes of Scout and Jem Finch, Harper Lee explores with rich humor and unswerving honesty the irrationality of adult attitudes toward race and class in the Deep South of the 1930s.

Lubar, David. Sleeping Freshmen Never Lie. Dutton Juvenile, 2005. (Grades 8-10)

⁓ A humorous account of an awkward freshman boy who's going after the girl. To top it off, his mom is pregnant.

Marshall, Catherine. Christy. Avon Books, 1983. (Grades 7-12)

⁓ At nineteen, Christy Huddleston left home to teach school in the Smokies --- coming to know and care for the wild mountain people, with their fierce pride, terrible poverty dark superstitions... and their yearning for beauty and truth. But in these primitive surrounding, Christy's faith would be severely tested by the unique strengths and needs of two remarkable young men --- and challenged by a heart torn between desire... and love.

Marshall, Paule. Brown Girl, Brownstones. Feminist Press, 1996. (Grades 7-12)

⁓ Somewhat autobiographical, this groundbreaking work describes the coming of age of Selina Boyce, a Caribbean-American girl in New York City in the mid-20th century.

McCullers, Carson. The Heart is a Lonely Hunter. Bantam Books, 1983. (Grades 9 and up)

⁓ The heroine is the strange young girl, Mick Kelly. The setting is a small Southern town. The characters are the damned, the voiceless, the rejected. Somefight their loneliness with violence and depravity, Some with sex or drink, and some -- like Mick -- with a quiet, intensely personal search for beauty.

McCullers, Carson. The Member of the Wedding. Bantam Books, 1985. (Grades 9 and up)

⁓ Twelve-year-old Frankie Adams, longing at once for escape and belonging, takes her role as "member of the wedding" to mean that when her older brother marries she will join the happy couple in their new life together. But Frankie is unlucky in love; her mother is dead, and Frankie narrowly escapes being raped by a drunken soldier during a farewell tour of the town. Worst of all, "member of the wedding" doesn't mean what she thinks. This is a brief coming-of-age novel.

Mishima, Yukio. The Sound of Waves. Vintage Books USA, 1994. (Grades 8 and up)
~ The book starts when a young and poor fisherman, Shinji, coming back from his work, catches a sight of a beautiful girl, Hatsue, a daughter of the wealthiest man in the village. The two young people meet and fall in love with each other for the first time in their lives. As they set out on adventure of experiencing all joys of their feelings they also have to overcome all the difficulties their life presents them.

Myracle, Lauren. Eleven. Puffin, 2008. (Grades 4-6)
~ Winne experiences all the ups and downs of growing up, especially all the trials that are associated with fickle friends.

Myracle, Lauren. Twelve. Puffin, 2008. (Grades 5-7)
~ Everything about this age is addressed; from the physical changes of the body to all the changes in friendships.

Myracle, Lauren. Thirteen. Puffin, 2008 (Grades 6-8)
~ The growth of Winnie continues as interest in boys escalates. . . as do her troubles with her "BFFs."

Salinger, J.D. Catcher in the Rye. Little, Brown, 1991. (Grades 9 and up)
~ This story details the two days in the life of 16-year-old Holden Caulfield after he has been expelled from prep school. Confused and disillusioned, he searches for truth and rails against the "phoniness" of the adult world. He ends up exhausted and emotionally ill, in a psychiatrist's office. After he recovers from his breakdown, Holden relates his experiences to the reader.

Toth, Susan Allen. Blooming: A Small-Town Girlhood. Ballantine Books, 1989.
~ Slumber parties, swimming pools, boyfriends, lakeside summers, family holidays -- Susan Allen Toth has captured it all in this account of growing up in Ames, Iowa, in the 1950s. Blooming celebrates an innocent and very American way of life.

Twain, Mark. The Adventures of Huckleberry Finn. Penguin Books, 2003. (Grades 7-12)
~ A young teenage boy and an escaped slave travel down the Mississippi River with nothing but a raft and an obscure plan about how to change their lives.

Villasenor, Victor. Macho. Delta Trade Paperbacks, 1997. (Grades 9-12)

~ Dreaming of freedom, wealth, and respect, young Roberto Garcia crosses the Mexican border into California, where he experiences difficult culture shock but comes into his own as a man.

Wolfe, Tobias. The Boy's Life. Grove Press, 2000. (Grades 7-12)
~ Separated by divorce from his father and brother, Toby and his mother are constantly on the move, yet they develop an extraordinarily close, almost telepathic relationship. Toby fights for identity and self-respect against the unrelenting hostility of a new stepfather.

Zindel, Paul. The Pigman. Starfire, 1983. (Grades 8 and up)
~ Loraine and John learn a lot about themselves from the once victim of their phone prank, the Pigman. Up to this point, they've struggled to find any meaning in their lives.

Handicaps/Overcoming Handicaps

Byers, Betsy. <u>The Summer of the Swans</u>. Viking, 1970. (Grades 4-8)
  - A teen-aged girl gains insight into her priorities when her mentally challenged brother becomes lost.

Cairo, Shelley. <u>Our Brother has Down's Syndrome</u>. Annick, 1985. (Grades 4-8)
  - Children are introduced to Jai, and discover that the differences between them and him are not so great.

Clifton, Lucille. <u>My Friend Jacob</u>. Dutton, 1980. (Grades 4-8)
  - A young boy tells about Jacob, who though older and mentally challenged, is his best friend.

Gibson, William. <u>The Miracle Worker</u>. Pocket, 2002. (Grades 6-12)
  - Twelve-year-old Helen Keller lived in a prison of silence and darkness. Born deaf, blind, and mute, with no way to express herself or comprehend those around her, she flew into primal rages against anyone who tried to help her, fighting tooth and nail with a strength born of furious, unknowing desperation. Then Annie Sullivan came. Half-blind herself, but possessing an almost fanatical determination, she would begin a frightening and incredibly moving struggle to tame the wild girl no one could reach, and bring Helen into the world at last.

Greenberg, Joanne. <u>I Never Promised You a Rose Garden</u>. Signet Book, 1984. (Grades 6-12)

~ Chronicles the three-year battle of a mentally ill, but perceptive, teenage girl against a world of her own creation, emphasizing her relationship with the doctor who gave her the ammunition of self-understanding with which to help herself.

Gunther, John. Death Be Not Proud. Perennial, 1998. (Grades 9-12)
~ This true story relates a father's recollection of his son's courageous and spirited battle against the brain tumor that would take his life at the age of seventeen.

Hampshire, Susan. Susan's Story. St Martins Pr, 1983. (Grades 7-12)
~ This autobiographical story tells of Susan's struggles as a girl making her way up to the top as a dyslexic actress. It also describes dyslexic children, and how to help.

Keats, Ezra Jack. Apt. 3. Macmillan, 1973. (Grades 7-12)
~ Two brothers search for a harmonica player in their apartment building. When they find him, they discover he is blind, but has used his ears to learn a great deal about the world.

Keyes, Daniel. Flowers for Algernon. Harvest Books, 2004. (Grades 7-12)
~ The story of a mentally disabled man whose experimental quest for intelligence mirrors that of Algernon, an extraordinary lab mouse. In poignant diary entries, Charlie tells how a brain operation increases his IQ and changes his life. As the experimental procedure takes effect, Charlie's intelligence expands until it surpasses that of the doctors who engineered his metamorphosis. The experiment seems to be a scientific breakthrough of paramount importance-until Algernon begins his sudden, unexpected deterioration. Will the same happen to Charlie?

Maclachlan, Patricia. Through Grandpa's Eyes. Harper & Row, 1980. (Grades 4-8)
~ A young boy learns a different way of seeing the world from his blind grandpa.

Rabe, Bernice. The Balancing Girl. Dutton, 1981. (Grades 4-8)
~ Margaret balances well in her wheelchair, and on her crutches. She balances magic markers and cans for teachers. When she balances dominoes for the school fair, everyone sees her skills.

Valens, E.G. The Other Side of the Mountain. HarperCollins, 1989. (Grades 7-12)
~ Jill was an Olympic skiing star. In one of the last skiing races before she and others could try out for the Olympics, she had a serious

accident. The crash left her paralyzed from the shoulders down. After finding this out, Jill had another sort of mountain to climb. It was from being able to do absolutely nothing to going back to a meaningful way of life again.

Voigt, Cynthia. <u>Izzy Willy Nilly</u>. Atheneum, 1986. (Grades 6-12)

~ Izzy, a junior in high school, is devastated when she loses the lower half of her leg in an accident. Her loss is further compounded by the lack of caring from her three closest friends. Izzy learned to face her feeling and understand the true meaning of friendship.

Werlin, Nancy. <u>Are You Alone on Purpose?</u> Houghton Mifflin Company, 1994. (Grades 7-12)

~ Thirteen-year-old Alison Shandling has always been the good child: calming her autistic twin brother, deflecting her mother's rage, and pleasing her aloof father. Harry Roth has always been the cool kid who tests everyone's limits, especially those of his widowed father, the town's rabbi. The two dislike each other at first sight. When an accident confines Harry to a wheelchair, Alison recognizes his frustration and loneliness and initiates a friendship.

Homosexuality

Bass, Ellen and Kaufman, Kate. Free Your Mind: The Book for Gay, Lesbian & Bisexual Youth & Their Allies. Perennial Currents, 1996. (Grades 9 and up)
   ~ This book examines the basic aspects of the lives of gay, lesbian, and bisexual youth: self-discovery, friends and lovers, family, school, spirituality, and community.

Bauer, Marion Dane. Am I Blue? : Coming Out from the Silence. HarperTrophy, 1995. (Grades 7 and up)
   ~ A collection of short stories about homosexuality by such authors as Bruce Coville, M.E. Kerr, William Sleator, and Jane Yolen.

Brown, Rita Mae. Rubyfruit Jungle. Bantam Books, 1983. (Grades 10 and up)
   ~ The book tells the story of a lower-class girl growing up, her learning about sex and dealing with her own homosexuality, leaving home and starting a life of her own, college, city life, dating, etc. The reader identifies with Molly through all of her hardships and celebrates with her through her joyous relationships. This book deals with lesbianism in a very realistic manner, but at the same time could appeal to heterosexual women and men of all types.

Desetta, Al, M.A. and Wolin, Sybil, Ph.D. The Struggle to Be Strong True Stories by Teens About Overcoming Tough Times. Free Spirit Publishing. (Grades 7 and up)
   ~ In 30 first-person accounts, teens tell how they overcame major life obstacles, including, drug abuse by loved ones, interracial relationships, abandonment, homosexuality, and more.

Frost, Helen. <u>Keesha's House</u>. Farrar, Straus, and Giroux, 2003. (Grades 9 and up)

~ Joe's mother died when he was young. His aunt took him in when he was 12, and he now owns that house. Keesha's dad is a mean drunk so Joe takes her in. Also in the book is a pregnant 16 year old, a young man whose father threw him out because he is gay, a victim of sexual abuse, a child who's been abandoned then ends up in juvie, and a child whose parents are in jail.

Garden, Nancy. <u>Annie On My Mind</u>. Aerial, 1992. (Grades 7-12)

~ Garden's tale concerns two teenage girls who fall in love with each other. It is the story of two young women who love each other. It is an honest portrayal of their love.

Garden, Nancy. <u>The Year They Burned Books</u>. Farrar, Strauss, and Giroux, 1999. (Grades 9-12).

~ Controversy begins with an open editorial in the school newspaper, condoning the distribution of condoms. Jamie's realization that she's gay adds to the issues addressed in this book.

Gravelle, Karen, et al. <u>What's Going on Down There: Answers to Questions Boys Find Hard to Ask</u>. Walker & Company, 1998. (Grades 9 and up)

~ Describes the physical and emotional changes that occur in boys (and, to a lesser extent, in girls) during puberty and discusses sexual activity, homosexuality, AIDS, and other related topics.

Heron, Ann. <u>How Would You Feel if Your Dad was Gay?</u> Alyson Wonderland, 1994. (Grades 2-6)

~ Jasmine thinks she's lucky to have three dads--a stepfather, her natural father, and his lover. However, her schoolmates and even teachers find this hard to accept. Jasmine's brother is subjected to name-calling and almost ends up in a fight over his father's lifestyle. At home, the two dads are supportive and understanding, and the children's natural father contacts the principal about it. A special assembly is the result, with a children's counselor discussing different kinds of families. A subplot, featuring a lesbian and her son, speaks nonjudgmentally to the issue of the sexual preferences among the offspring of homosexual parents

Huegel, Kelly. <u>GLBTQ: The Survival Guide for Queer and Questioning Teens.</u> Free Spirit Publishing. (Grades 7 and up)

~ Topics addressed include: coming out, facing prejudice and pressure, getting support, navigating relationships, staying safe, making healthy choices, surviving and thriving in high school, and more. First hand experience guides the reader to accept him/herself.

Klein, Norma. Breaking Up. Random House Childrens Books, 1980. (Grades 9-12)

~ While she is visiting her father and stepmother in California, 15-year-old Alison learns her mother is a lesbian.

Larson, Rodger. What I Know. Henry Holt & Co., 1987. (Grades 7 and up)

~ It is 1957 and Dave Ryan, a lonely 14-year-old boy living with his newly divorced mother, is wishing he had more friends and a closer relationship with his dad. When his mother hires Gene Tole to refurbish a garden in their new house, Dave discovers emotions he never imagined. The book recounts the exhilaration of first love as Dave becomes more and more attached to Gene. Dave has little idea that homosexuality even exists.

Muharrar, Aisha. More Than a Label Why What You Wear or Who You're With Doesn't Define Who You Are. Free Spirit Publishing. (Grades 6 – 12)

~ Written from the viewpoint of the 17-year-old author, various labels and how to deal with them are discussed. Also addressed are cliques, peer pressure, popularity, racism, sexism, and homophobia. This book empowers students and shows them how to assert their self-worth.

Palardy, Debra J. Sweetie Here's the Best Reason on the Planet to Say No to Your Boyfriend: Even If You've Already Said Yes. Dorrance Pub Co, 2000. (Grades 8 and up)

~ This book is for adolescents who may have felt pressured to engage in activities in which they were not always comfortable or completely willing. It addresses the issue of changing morals in schools and concerns that this may be enough to make even the most straight-laced young lady feel that sexual activity is okay. Author Debra J. Palardy presents a collection of lines used by hormone-driven teenage boys to get their girlfriends to engage in sex. She follows through and provides useful comeback and advice for girls, considering their boyfriends' pleas. The author provides the objective wisdom sought by teenagers too embarrassed, timid, or afraid to consult those closet to them. Her guide points out the pitfalls of becoming sexually active, including pregnancy, sexually transmitted disease, and loss of self-esteem. She urges teenage girls to seek guidance from women who have had the time to develop an adult perspective and look back on their own experiences.

Ponton, Lynn, MD. <u>The Sex Lives of Teenagers: Revealing the Secret World of Adolescent Boys and Girls</u>. Plume Books, 2001. (Grades 9 and up)
~ With more and more teenagers having sex by the age of sixteen and others feeling pressured to before they're ready, parents and adolescents must find ways to communicate openly and honestly about a subject that has been ignored for too long. Lynn Ponton, M.D., takes a look at what teenagers have to say about their sexual lives. In a safe forum, without fear of judgment or censorship, teens feel free to speak frankly about their feelings, desires, fantasies, and expectations. And parents give voice to the struggle of coming to terms with their children's emerging sexual identities.   Dr. Ponton opens a dialogue that addresses controversial topics such as pregnancy, abortion, masturbation, sexual orientation, Internet dating, and gender roles. Sensitive subjects such as AIDS and drugs are also explored.

Revoyr, Nina. <u>The Necessary Hunger: A Novel</u>. Simon & Schuster, 1997. (Grades 9-12)
~ As a star basketball player in her last year of high school, Nancy Takahiro's life is about to change forever. Faced with the college recruitment process and unsure of where her skill will take her, Nancy is not prepared for meeting Raina Webber, an All-State shooting star. When Nancy's father and Raina's mother move in together, the girls are faced with the challenge of negotiating their already intense friendship and rivalry. As Nancy's love for Raina grows and both prepare to leave inner city neighborhood, they find themselves looking toward a future that is no longer easily defined.

Sanchez, Alex. <u>Rainbow Boys</u>. Simon Pulse, 2003. (Grades 9 and up)
~ Three high school seniors, a jock with a girlfriend and an alcoholic father, a closeted gay, and a flamboyant gay rights advocate, struggle with family issues, gay bashers, first sex, and conflicting feelings about each other.

Scoppetone, Sandra. <u>Happy Endings Are All Alike</u>. Alyson Publications, 2000. (Grades 9-12)
~ Small town prejudices emerge when a love affair between two teenage girls is revealed.

Snow, Judith. <u>How It Feels to Have a Gay or Lesbian Parent: A Book by Kids for Kids of All Ages</u>. Harrington Park Press, 2004. (Grades 5-8)
- Thirty-two first-hand accounts from people of all ages on what it is/was like to have a parent who is homosexual.

Swisher, Karin L., Leone, Bruno, and O'Neil, Terry. <u>Teenage Sexuality: Opposing Viewpoints</u>. Gale Group, 1994. (Grades 9 and up)
- An examination of birth control, sex education, STDs, homosexuality, pregnancy, and changes in the attitudes toward teenage sexuality and morality. The book explores a wide range of opinions and perspectives. *(Doris A. Fong)*

Ure, Jean. <u>Other Side of the Fence</u>. Bantam Doubleday Dell, 1992. (Grades 8-12)
- Class lines, sexual preferences, and economic differences are torn apart when Bonny hitches a ride from Richard. Bonny, dumped by her boyfriend Jake, and Richard, kicked out of his house by his father, shack up together in an abandoned house. Both get jobs, and they spend four weeks together. An acquaintance drops hints that Jake has returned from his musical jaunt to Ireland and Bonny runs back to him immediately, relinquishing all of her cash and self-respect. Jake's sarcasm and belittling force Bonny to take stock of her life, and she returns to Richard who's back at college and finally able to accept his homosexuality.

Walker, Kate. <u>Peter</u>. Houghton Mifflin Company, 2001. (Grades 7-12)
- Pressured by his peers and society to conform to the stereotyped macho image, fifteen-year-old Peter feels both confused and repelled. His confusion and his horror increase when he finds himself attracted to his brother's best friend, David, who is gay.

Illness

Beckman, Gunnel. <u>Admission to the Feast</u>. Holt, Rinehart and Winston, 1972. (Grades 9-12)
- A nineteen-year-old girl, dying of leukemia, writes a long letter to a friend in an attempt to stabilize her crumbling world.

Lowry, Lois. <u>Summer to Die</u>. Laurel Leaf, 1984. (Grades 7-12)
- Thirteen-year-old Meg envies her sister's beauty and popularity. Her feelings don't make it any easier for her to cope with Molly's strange illness and eventual death from leukemia.

Pople, Maureen. <u>Road to Summering</u>. University of Queensland Press, 1990. (Grades 9-12)
- Deals with an individual in a coma.

Rubalcaba, Jill. <u>Saint Vitus' Dance</u>. Clarion Books, 1996. (Grades 6-10)
- The tough and touching story of Melanie, whose mother has Huntington's chorea, and her coming to terms with her feelings about a cruel and tragic disease.

Slepian, Jan. <u>Alfred Summer</u>. Simon & Schuster Children's, 1980. (Grades 6-12)
- It all started when Lester saved Alfred's life. Neither of the boys-Lester with cerebral palsy or mentally challenged Alfred-has ever had a real friend before. Then they're joined by gentle giant Myron, and Claire, the tomboy. The four band together to work on the rowboat Myron is building in his basement-and, as they do, they learn about each other, friendship, and the world.

Sones, Sonya. <u>Stop Pretending</u>. HarperTempest, 2001. (Grades 7-12)
- This book is about a 13-year-old girl whose older sister goes crazy and is admitted into a mental institution. When the younger sister goes to visit her, she is doing all kinds of crazy things and is a totally different person.

Southall, Ivan. <u>Let the Balloon Go</u>. Methuen, 1969. (Grades 9-12)
- Handicapped by cerebral palsy and overprotected by his parents, a twelve-year-old, left alone for the first time, in a desperate need to exert his independence, does precisely what he has been forbidden to do.

Strasser, Todd. <u>Friends Till the End</u>. Laurel Leaf Books, 1981. (Grades 6-12)
- David befriended a nerd and has to deal with peer pressure as he supports hisnew friend throughout his agonizing struggle with leukemia.

Individuality/Responsibility

Alexander, Ruth Bell. <u>Changing Bodies, Changing Lives: A Book for Teens on Sex and Relationships</u>. Three Rivers Press, 1998. (Grades 8 and up)
~ *Changing Bodies, Changing Lives* has helped teenagers make informed decisions about their lives, from questions about sex, love, friendship, and how your body works to dealing with problems at school and home and figuring out who you are.

Avi. <u>Nothing But the Truth</u>. HarperTrophy, 1993. (Grades 5-9)
~ Ninth-grade student Philip Malloy was suspended from school for singing along to *The Star-Spangled Banner* in his homeroom, causing what his teacher, Margaret Narwin, called "a disturbance." But was he standing up for his patriotic ideals, only to be squelched by the school system? Was Ms. Narwin simply trying to be a good teacher? Or could it all be just a misunderstanding gone bad -- very bad?

Bauer, Marion D. <u>On My Honor</u>. Yearling Books, 1987. (Grades 5-9)
~ Twelve-year-old Joel has unwillingly agreed to bike out to the state park with his daredevil friend Tony. "On his honor," he promises his father to be careful, knowing that Tony wants them to climb the dangerous park bluffs. When they arrive, however, Tony abruptly changes his mind and heads for the river. With his promise jangling in his mind, Joel follows Tony in for a swim. Tony drowns in the dirty, turbulent water, leaving Joel to face his guilty conscience, and his father, alone....

Feiffer, Jules. <u>The Man in the Ceiling</u>. Harper Collins, 1993. (Grades 5-10)

~ Jimmy, a cartoonist, turns his back on his creativity to achieve popularity. Gradually, he learns to trust his talent.

Graham, John. It's Up to Us The Giraffe Heroes Program for Teens. Free Spirit Publishing. (Grades 7 and up)
~ Written to encourage meaning, courage, compassion and personal responsibility in the lives of young adults.

Harrison, Lisi. The Clique. Little, Brown, 2004. (Grades 6-10)
~ This book is all about 7th grade girls who have to learn what to wear and what to do to fit in. Claire gets made fun of because she doesn't fit in the rich community she just moved to.

Lewis, Barbara A. What Do You Stand For? A Kid's Guide to Building Character. Free Spirit Press. (Grades 5 and up)
~ This book invites kids to explore and practice honesty, kindness, empathy, integrity, tolerance, patience, respect, and more. Scenarios are set up to help children decide what they'd do.

Lowry, Lois. The Giver. Laurel Leaf, 2002. (Grades 6-10)
~ In a world with no poverty, no crime, no sickness and no unemployment, and where every family is happy, 12-year-old Jonas is chosen to be the community's Receiver of Memories. Under the direction of the Elders and an old man known as the Giver, he discovers the disturbing truth about his utopian world and struggles against the weight of its hypocrisy. Lowry examines the idea that people might freely choose to give up their humanity in order to create a more stable society. Gradually Jonas learns just how costly this ordered and pain-free society can be, and boldly decides he cannot pay the price.

Mirriam-Goldberg, Caryn, PhD. Write Where You Are How to Use Writing to Make Sense of Your Life. Free Spirit Publishing. (Grades 7 and up)
~ Write Where You Are helps teens use writing to better understand themselves and where they're going in life.

Spinelli, Jerry. Stargirl. Knopf Books for Young Readers, 2002. (Grades 6-12)
~ In this story about the perils of popularity, the courage of nonconformity, and the thrill of first love, an eccentric student named Stargirl changes Mica High School forever.

Internet Safety

Bailey, Diane. <u>Cyber Ethics</u>. The Rosen Publishing Group Incorporated, 2008. (Grades 6 and up).
-Includes Internet safety, glossary of terms, and safety tips. This book helps its readers stay up-to-date with the latest on the Internet, and also provides information to keep its users safe.

Courtney, Vicky. <u>Teenvirtue: Real Issues, Real Life. . . A Teen Girl's Survival Guide</u>. B&H Publishing Group, 2005. (Grades 6-12)
- Offers Christian advice for issues such as: friendships, boys, fashion and beauty, and heavier issues such as Internet safety, sex and drugs. The format is not "preachy," but resembles that of popular magazines.

Farnham, Kevin and Farnham, Dale. <u>MySpace Safety: 51 Tips for Teens and Parents How-to-Primers</u>, 2006. (Grades 7 and up)
- This book is meant to help kids understand and be safe on MySpace. Issues addressed include how to get an account, how to report inappropriate posts, and most importantly, how to stay safe.

Fine, Lawrence. <u>Online Lifeline: Internet Safety for Kids . . . and their Parents.</u> Profits Publishing, 2007. (Grades 7-12)
- Addresses all the uses for the Internet and emphasizes the safety steps along the way.

Ikeepsafe, and Linford, Sally. <u>Faux Paw's Adventures in the Internet: Keeping Kids Safe</u>. Wiley, John and Sons, Incorporated, 2006. (Grades 2-8)

~ Addresses Internet safety in a kid-friendly and interesting manner.

Newsome, Tony. <u>High School Student Safety Tips</u>. Carrington Books, 2007. (Grades 8-12)
~ Includes tips from an LA police officer intended to keep high school students safe. This book includes ideas to keep these kids safe on the Internet as well as other safety and prevention techniques.

Newsome, Tony. <u>Middle School Student Safety Tips</u>. Carrington Books, 2007. (Grades 5-8)
~ Teaches middle school students how to stay safe. Tips include how to stay safe from predators, strangers, and on the Internet, as well as other prevention techniques to stay safe. All these tips come from an LA police officer with 27 years of experience.

Schwartau, Winn. <u>Internet and Computer Ethics for Kids: (and Parents & Teachers Who Haven't Got a Clue)</u>. Interpact Press, 2001. (Grades 6 and up)
~ Schwartau uses humor to teach kids (and parents and teachers) about computer Ethics and Internet safety.

Sommers, Michael. <u>Dangers of Online Predators</u>. The Rosen Publishing Group, Incorporated, 2008. (Grades 10 and up)
~ Includes the dangers of, and how to stay clear of cyber predators. The book includes real stories of online predators.

Learning Challenges

Abeel, Samantha. My Thirteenth Winter: A Memoir. Scholastic, Inc., 2003. (Grades 6-12)
~ Samantha Abeel tells her own story of living with and overcoming dyscalculia. She describes in painstaking detail how her life was affected by her learning disability before and after she was diagnosed, and the way her peers, her family, and her teachers treated her. In seventh grade, Samantha suffered anxiety attacks as she struggled to keep up in her classes, to remember two locker combinations, and to deal with new teachers. Samantha was eventually placed in Special Education classes in eighth grade, but she continued to feel anxious about her future.

Abeel, Samantha. Reach for the Moon. Scholastic, Inc., 2001. (Grades 6-12)
~ Poetry, written by a girl with learning disabilities, reflects her feelings and experiences.

Andrews, Jean F. Flying Fingers Club. Gallaudet University Press, 1988. (Grades 6-12)
~ Entering a new school, Donald struggles with his learning disability and makes friends with a deaf boy who teaches him sign language and joins Donald in a search for a newspaper thief.

Cummings, Rhoda, Ed.D. and Fisher, Gary, Ph.D. The Survival Guide for Teenagers with LD (Learning Differences). Free Spirit Publishing. (Grades 7 and up)

~ This guide helps young people with learning challenges succeed in school and prepare for life as adults. Also included is assertiveness, jobs, friends, dating, self-sufficiency, and responsible citizenship.

DeClements, Barthe. Sixth Grade Can Really Kill You. Penguin Group (USA), 1985. (Grades 5-8)
~ Helen fears that lack of improvement in her reading may leave her stuck in the sixth grade forever, until a good teacher recognizes her reading problem.

Fisher, Gary L., Cummings, Rhonda W., and Espeland, Pamela. School Survival Guide for Kids with LD (Learning Differences): Ways to Make Learning Easier and More Fun. Free Spirit Publishing, Inc., 1991. (Grades 6-12)
~ Strategies and tips for building confidence in reading, writing, spelling, and math, managing time, coping with testing, getting help, and more.

Fisher, Gary L. and Cummings, Rhoda. The Survival Guide for Kids with LD. Free Spirit Publishing, Inc., 2002. (Grades 6-12)
~ Discusses how children with "learning differences" can get along better in school, set goals, and plan for the future. Goldish, Meish.

Everything You Need to Know about Dyslexia. Rosen Publishing Group, 1998. (Grades 6-12)
~ Explains the causes and symptoms of dyslexia and discusses how to overcome this disability and become a good reader and writer.

Hall, Lynn. Just One Friend. Simon & Schuster Children's, 1985. (Grades 6-12)
~ Just as sixteen-year-old learning-disabled Doreen is about to be mainstreamed into a regular school, the loss of her best friend to another girl drives her to a desperate act.

Hampshire, Susan. Susan's Story. St Martins Pr, 1983. (Grades 7-12)
~ This autobiographical story tells of Susan's struggles as a girl making her way up to the top as a dyslexic actress. It also describes dyslexic children, and how to help.

Jenkins, A. M. Out of Order. HarperTeen, 2003. (Grades 8-10)
~ Struggling with academics, the sports star, Colt seeks help in a tutor to help save his image.

Philbrick, Rodman R. and Philbrick, W.R. Freak the Mighty. Scholastic, Inc., 2001. (Grades 6-10)

~ At the beginning of eighth grade, learning disabled Max and his new friend Freak, whose birth defect has affected his body but not his brilliant mind, find that when they combine forces they make a powerful team.

Rubin, Susan Goldman. Emily Good as Gold. Harcourt, 1993. (Grades 6-12)
~ Emily Gold, a learning disabled thirteen-year-old, struggles to be independent from her overprotective parents.

Slepian, Jan. Alfred Summer. Simon & Schuster Children's, 1980. (Grades 6-12)
~ It all started when Lester saved Alfred's life. Neither of the boys-Lester with cerebral palsy or mentally challenged Alfred-has ever had a real friend before. Then they're joined by gentle giant Myron, and Claire, the tomboy. The four band together to work on the rowboat Myron is building in his basement-and, as they do, they learn about each other, friendship, and the world.

Williams, James M. Out to Get Jack. Trafford Publishing, 2003. (Grades 6-12)
~ Jack Lack is a mainstreamed eleven-year-old with high-functioning autism. Because he can "talk and did well on spelling tests," he doesn't qualify for the sanctuary of the autism classroom, but instead has been thrown into the BD/JD [behavior-disordered/juvenile delinquent] classroom, which is full of wise-cracking kids. Jack is the only one who doesn't constantly misbehave, but because he lacks social skills, he is the one who is invariably blamed for everyone else's misdeeds.

Willis, Jeanne. Naked Without a Hat. Delacorte Press, 2004. (Grades 6-12)
~ Promising to keep his mother's secret, eighteen-year-old Will moves into a house for people with disabilities, falls in love with a young Gypsy woman, and learns to assert his own identity and independence.

Winkler, Henry and Oliver, Lin. Niagara Falls, Or Does It? (Hank Zipzer Series #1).Grosset & Dunlap, 2003. (Grades 4-6).
~ Inspired by his own experiences with undiagnosed dyslexia, actor/director Henry Winkler presents this new series about the high-spirited and funny adventures of a fourth-grader with learning differences. When Hank Zipzer has to write an essay on what he did over the summer, he decides instead to "show" what he did.

Male Bonding, A Need For

Strasser, Todd. <u>Friends Till the End</u>. Laurel Leaf Books, 1981. (Grades 6-12)
- David befriended a nerd and has to deal with peer pressure as he supports his new friend throughout his agonizing struggle with leukemia.

Voigt, Cynthia. <u>Sons From Afar</u>. Fawcett Juniper, 1987. (Grades 6-12)
- A search for a father forces two brothers to learn their strengths and weaknesses as well as powerful knowledge about themselves.

Moving

Blume, Judy. Then Again, Maybe I Won't. Bantam Doubleday Dell Books for Young Readers, 1981. (Grades 5-8)

~ Ever since his dad got rich from an invention and his family moved to a wealthy neighborhood on Long Island, Tony Miglione's life has been turned upside down. For starters, there's his new friend Joel, who shoplifts. Then there's Joel's sixteen-year-old sister, Lisa, who gets undressed every night without pulling down her shades. And there's Grandma, who won't come down from her bedroom. On top of all his other worries, Tony has questions about growing up... Why couldn't things have stayed the same?

Caswell, Brian. Mike. University of Queensland Press, 1993. (Grades 5-8)

~ When a twelve-year-old Australian moves with his mother to Sydney, he is victimized by a bully at school and befriended by a neighbor who has a secret to share.

Colfer, Eoin. Benny and Omar. O'Brien Press, Limited, The, 2001. (Grades 6-12)

~ Two cultures meet in this hilarious book about a young sports fanatic named Benny who is forced to leave his home in Ireland and move with his family to Tunisia. He wonders how he will survive in such an unfamiliar place. Then he teams up with wild and resourceful Omar, and a friendship between the two boys leads to trouble, escapades, a unique way of communicating, and ultimately a heartbreaking challenge.

Gantos, Jack. <u>Jack on the Tracks: Four Seasons of Fifth Grade</u>. Farrar, Straus and Giroux, 2001. (Grades 5-8)
~ After moving with his unbearable sister to Miami, Florida, Jack tries to breaksome of his bad habits but finds himself irresistibly drawn to things disgusting, gross, and weird.

Spence, Eleanor. <u>Nothing Place</u>. Harpercollins Juvenile Books, 1973. (Grades 9-12)
~ Learning to accept his partial deafness is bad enough, but having to adjust to a new neighborhood and a bunch of do-good friends is almost too much for Glen.

Telgemeier, Raina and Martin, Ann Matthew (Creator). <u>Truth About Stacy</u> (Baby-Sitters Club Series #2). Scholastic, Inc., 2006. (Grades 4-7)
~ Stacy not only has to deal with her diabetes diagnosis, her family just moved to a new town. Thankfully, she is able to make new friends who understand her disease.

Waber, Bernard. <u>Ira Says Good-Bye</u>. Houghton-Mifflin, 1988. (Grades 6-10)
~ Ira is surprised and hurt that his best friend is excited about moving to another town.

Wallace, Bill. <u>Aloha Summer</u>. Simon & Schuster Children's, 2000. (Grades 5-9)
~ In 1925, fourteen-year-old John, an Oklahoma farm boy, has to accept many changes in his life when his father takes a job on a pineapple plantation in Hawaii and the family moves there.

Yep, Laurence. <u>Star Fisher</u>. Puffin, 1992. (Grades 6-12)
~ Fifteen-year-old Joan Lee and her family find the adjustment hard when they move from Ohio to West Virginia in the 1920s.

Obsessive Compulsive Disorder

Bayer, Linda N. <u>Uneasy Lives: Understanding Anxiety Disorder.</u> Chelsea House Publishers, 2000. (Grades 7 and up)
~ Examines various anxiety disorders, including panic attacks, phobias, agoraphobia, obsessive-compulsive disorder, and post-traumatic stress.

Foster, Constance H. <u>Funny, You Don't Look Crazy: Life with Obsessive-Compulsive Disorder.</u> Dilligaf Publishing, 1994. (Grades 9 and up)
~ Five to eight million people, one out of 50 adults, struggle with obsessive-compulsive disorder. OCD sneaks up when it's least expected. Beginning with a description of the different types of obsessions and compulsions and the relationship between the disorder and genetics, this nonmedical book is filled with personal vignettes of how people and their families coped with this chronic illness.

Hesser, Terry Spencer. <u>Kissing Doorknobs</u>. Bantam Doubleday Dell Books for Young Readers, 1999. (Grades 9 and up)
~ Fourteen-year-old Tara describes how her increasingly strange compulsions begin to take over her life and affect her relationships with her family and friends.

Sebastian, Richard and Snyder, Solomon H. (Editor). <u>Compulsive Behavior.</u> Chelsea House Publishers, 1993. (Grades 7 and up)
~ An examination of compulsive behavior, focusing on the causes, effects, and treatment of this disorder.

Tashijan, Janet. <u>Multiple Choice</u>. Henry Holt & Company, Incorporated, 1999. (Grades 8 and up)

~ For as long as Monica Devon can remember, she has been two things: a whiz at making anagrams and a perfectionist who obsesses about saying and doing the right thing. Seeing no other way out from her compulsive nature, she creates "Multiple Choice," a roulette word game that will force spontaneity into her life. At first the game is exciting, but soon it gets dangerous. Fortunately for Monica, help is closer than she thinks.

Peer Pressure

Brown, Lyn Mikel. <u>Girlfighting: Betrayal and Rejection Among Girls</u>. New York University Press, 2003. (Grades 7 and up)
- Brown asserts girls are discouraged from expressing strong feelings and are pressured to fulfill unrealistic expectations, to be popular, and struggle to find their way in a society that still reinforces narrow gender stereotypes. Under such pressure, in their frustration and anger, girls (often unconsciously) find it less risky to take out their fears and anxieties on other girls instead of challenging the way boys treat them, the way the media represents them, or the way the culture at large supports sexist practices.

Carlson, Melody. <u>Becoming Me: Diary of a Teenage Girl, Book 1</u>. Multnomah, 2000. (Grades 8-10)
- The story of a Christian girl's transition from childhood to womanhood. Issues addressed include: peer pressure, loyalty, conflict with parents, the longing for a boyfriend, and her own spirituality.

Cormier, Robert. <u>The Chocolate War</u>. Laurel Leaf, 1986. (Grades 8–12)
- Jerry Renault refuses to sell chocolates during his school's fundraiser and creates quite a stir. It's as if the whole school comes apart at the seams. To some, Jerry is a hero, but to others, he becomes a scapegoat--a target for their pent-up hatred. Jerry's just trying to stand up for what he believes in.

Courtney, Vicky. <u>Teenvirtue: Real Issues, Real Life. . . A Teen Girl's Survival Guide</u>. B&H Publishing Group, 2005. (Grades 6-12)

~ Offers Christian advice for issues such as: friendships, boys, fashion and   beauty, and heavier issues such as Internet safety, sex and drugs. The format is not "preachy," but resembles that of popular magazines.

Crutcher, Chris. Whale Talk. Laurel Leaf Books, 2002. (Grades 7 and up)
~ A group of misfits on a swim team with no pool try to find a way to fit in.

Dessen, Sarah. Keeping the Moon. Penguin USA, 2004. (Grades 6 and up)
~ Fifteen-year-old Colie has never fit in. First, it was because she was fat. Then, after she lost the weight, it was because of a reputation that she didn't deserve. So when she's sent to stay with her eccentric aunt Mira for the summer, Colie doesn't expect too much. After all, why would anyone in Colby, North Carolina, want to bother with her when no one back home does?

Feiffer, Jules. The Man in the Ceiling. Harper Collins, 1993. (Grades 5-10)
~ Jimmy, a cartoonist, turns his back on his creativity to achieve popularity. Gradually, he learns to trust his talent.

Flinn, Alex. Breaking Point. HarperTempest, 2003. (Grades 8 and up)
~ Fifteen-year-old Paul enters an exclusive private school and falls under the spell of a charismatic boy who may be using him.

Fredericks, Mariah. The True Meaning of Cleavage. Simon & Schuster Children's, 2004.
~ Frederick's portrays one ninth-grader's struggle with her friend becoming "the other girl." When Jess and Sari enter high school, the two buds fully expect the usual popularity contests that divide the "in" kids from the "out." This is a novel that helps teen readers take stock of their own pride and dignity (*Shana Taylor*).

Gallo, Donald R. On the Fringe. Puffin, 2003. (Grades 6 and up)
~ In every school at every grade, there's a pecking order among students-an in crowd and those outside it, who are often ridiculed mercilessly for the "crime" of being different. A tomboy finds the relief of self-expression through her music, while in another tale a relentless bully tests the faith of an intensely religious girl. A cheerleader discovers that the true soul of her school can't be found within the cool clique; a football player finally stands up for a

harassed fellow student; and a boy watches in horror as the school "freak" marches into his classroom with a loaded rifle.

Gardner, Graham. <u>Inventing Elliot</u>. Penguin Group (USA) Incorporated, 2004.(Grades 7-10)
  ⁓ Elliot, a victim of bullying, invents a calmer, cooler self when he changes schools in the middle of freshman year, but soon attracts the wrong kind of attention from the Guardians who "maintain order" at the new school.

Hall, Lynn. <u>Just One Friend</u>. Simon & Schuster Children's, 1985. (Grades 6-12)
  ⁓ Just as sixteen-year-old learning-disabled Doreen is about to be mainstreamed into a regular school, the loss of her best friend to another girl drives her to a desperate act.

Harrison, Lisi. <u>The Clique Series</u>. 2004-2007. (Grades 6-10)
  ⁓ This book is all about 7th grade girls who have to learn what to wear and what to do to fit in. Claire gets made fun of because she doesn't fit in the rich community she just moved to.

Klein, Robin. <u>All in the Blue Unclouded Weather</u>. Puffin, 1993. (Grades 9-12)
  ⁓ Poverty causes the Mellings to struggle with peer relationships.

Klein, Robin. <u>Hating Alison Ashley</u>. Trumpet Club, 1990. (Grades 7-12)
  ⁓ Erika Yurken thinks she is tops in her "socially disadvantaged school" until upperclass, golden girl Alison Ashley is enrolled. Erika is envious of the style and class Alison seems to have.

Korman, Gordon. <u>Jake, Reinvented</u>. Hyperion Books for Children, 2003. (Grades 7-12)
  ⁓ Jake Garett is a new student who like he just stepped off the cover of the J. Crew catalog. He's a football star and hosts a party every Friday night. All the guys want to be like him and all the girls want to date him. Through the eyes of Jake's friend, Rick, readers get to know Jake, first admiring him, then liking him, but eventually fearing for him as they learn Jake's secret.

Mosatche, Dr. Harriet S. , Unger, Karen, and Verdick, Elizabeth. <u>Too Old for This, Too Young for That!: Your Survival Guide for the Middle-School Years</u>. Free Spirit Publishing, Inc., 1999. (Grades 5-9)
  ⁓ Quizzes, stories, surveys, and activities for middle schoolers addressing such issues as physical and emotional changes, connecting with friends and family, setting goals, and handling peer pressure.

Muharrar, Aisha. <u>More Than a Label Why What You Wear or Who You're With Doesn't Define Who You Are</u>. Free Spirit Publishing. (Grades 6 – 12)
~ Written from the viewpoint of the 17-year-old author, various labels and how to deal with them are discussed. Also addressed are cliques, peer pressure, popularity, racism, sexism, and homophobia. This book empowers students and shows them how to assert their self-worth.

Rainey, Dennis, Barbara, Samuel, and Rebecca. <u>So You're About to Be a Teenager: Godly Advice for Preteens on Friends, Love, Sex, Faith and Other Life Issues</u>. Nelson Books, 2003. (Grades 6 and up)
~ Samuel and Rebecca Rainey share their perspective as young adults who recall their own successes and failures as teenagers. They cover the topics of friends, peer pressure, boundaries, dating, and sex. The Raineys address the most common traps of adolescence and teach young people how to avoid making poor choices.

Roehlkepartain, Jolene. <u>Surviving School Stress</u>. Group Pub Inc., 1990. (Grades 6-12)
~ Focuses on school-related stress and how to deal with it from a Christian perspective. Discusses grades, parents' expectations, after-school activities, and getting along with people who have different beliefs.

Rose, Reginald. <u>Twelve Angry Men</u>. Dramatic Publications, 1983. (Grades 9 and up)
~ This is a book about twelve jurors who have varied opinions on the issues involving a court case. They expected to come to a quick conclusion and it didn't happen. This is a book about sticking to your opinions whether someone else feels you are right are wrong.

Scott, Sharon. <u>How to Say No and Keep Your Friends: Peer Pressure Reversal for Teens and Preteens</u>. Human Resource Development Press, 1997. (Grades 5-12)
~ This book presents teens/preteens with very specific ways to manage all kinds of negative peer pressure--from gossip and cliques to the most serious problem invitations including drugs, sex, and even violence.

Spinelli, Jerry. <u>Stargirl</u>. Knopf Books for Young Readers, 2002. (Grades 6-12)
~ In this story about the perils of popularity, the courage of nonconformity, and the thrill of first love, an eccentric student named Stargirl changes Mica High School forever.

Strasser, Todd. <u>Friends Till the End</u>. Laurel Leaf Books, 1981. (Grades 6-12)

~ David befriended a nerd and has to deal with peer pressure as he supports hisnew friend throughout his agonizing struggle with leukemia.

Strasser, Todd and Rhue, Morton. <u>Wave</u>. Bantam Doubleday Dell Books for Young Readers, 1981. (Grades 7-12)

~ The powerful forces of group pressure that pervaded many historic movements such as Nazism are recreated in the classroom when history teacher Burt Ross introduces a "new" system to his students. And before long "The Wave," with its rules of "strength through discipline, community, and action," sweeps from the classroom through the entire school. And as most of the students join the movement, Laurie Saunders and David Collins recognize the frightening momentum of "The Wave" and realize they must stop it before it's too late.

Stewart, Bridgett, and White, Franklin. <u>No Matter What</u>. Blue/Black Press, 2002. (Grades 7-12)

~ Bridgett Stewart shares her journey through unthinkable poverty and discusses everything from gaining her own self-respect when no one else would respect her because of where she lived to surviving verbal abuse from classmates, living without a father, school pressures, and her decision to use education as a vehicle from poverty while earning a 4.0 grade point average in tough and trying times.Stewart also discusses self-esteem, alcohol and drugs, and many other topics.

Von Ziegesar, Cecily. <u>Gossip Girl</u>. Little, Brown & Company, 2002. (Grades 8-12)

~ Presents a world of jealousy and betrayal at an exclusive private school in Manhattan.

Williams, James M. <u>Out to Get Jack</u>. Trafford Publishing, 2003. (Grades 6-12)

~ Jack Lack is a mainstreamed eleven-year-old with high-functioning autism. Because he can "talk and did well on spelling tests," he doesn't qualify for the sanctuary of the autism classroom, but instead has been thrown into the BD/JD [behavior-disordered/juvenile delinquent] classroom, which is full of wise-cracking kids. Jack is the only one who doesn't constantly misbehave, but because he lacks social skills, he is the one who is invariably blamed for everyone else's misdeeds.

Physical Abuse

D'Amosio, Richard. No Language But a Cry. Doubleday, 1970. (Grades 9 and up)
- This is the true story of Dr. D'Ambrosio's struggle to help a battered child who has never spoken a word because of the physical abuse inflicted by her parents.

Dolan, Edward. Child Abuse. Watts, 1980. (Grades 7-12)
- The principle areas of child abuse, including physical and sexual abuse, are outlined.

Draper, Sharon. Forged By Fire. Simon Pulse, 1998. (Grades 6-12)
- This prequel to Draper's Tears of a Tiger is a portrayal of a young man struggling to protect his little sister from a drug-addicted mother and an abusive father.

Flinn, Alex. Breathing Underwater. HarperTempest, 2002. (Grade 9 and up)
- In this book, a girl named Cat is abused by her jealous boyfriend. Nick is only jealous because he loves Caitlin with all his heart. Partially because Nick was abused by his father, he doesn't know how else he should express his feelings. He truly loves Cat, but is also truly hurting her.

Haskins, James. The Child Abuse Help Book. Niles, Albert Whitman, 1981. (Grades 5-9)
- The problems that lead to and stem from child abuse accompany directionsfor help, including suggestions for personal action

Hyde, Margaret. Cry Softly: The Story of Child Abuse. Westminster, 1980. (Grades 7 and up)

~ Discusses child abuse, its history in England and America, ways to prevent and top it, and how to report suspected cases.

Kellogg, Majorie. Like the Lion's Tooth. Farrar, Straus, and Giroux, 1972. (Grades 5-9)
~ Eleven year old Ben, who has been physically and sexually abused by his father, is sent to school for "problem children." Ben eventually resigns himself to the situation.

Klass, David. You Don't Know Me. HarperTempest, 2002. (Grades 7 and up).
~ A 14-year-old describes the physical and emotional abuse from his mother's boyfriend. "The hero's underlying sense of isolation and thread of hope will strike a chord with nearly every adolescent" (Reed Business Information, Inc, 2002).

Mazer, Harry. The War on Villa Street. New York: Delacort, 1978. (Grades 5-9)
~ Willis, an eight year old, is frequently beaten by his alcoholic father. After striking back at his father, Willis runs away but returns, hoping things will improve.

Pelzer, David. A Child Called "It". Health Communications, 1995. (Grades 7 and up).
~ Pelzer describes the true story of how he was beaten by his mother and what steps were taken to overcome the abuse.

Pelzer, David. Help Yourself: Finding Hope, Courage, and Happiness. Plume, 2001. (Grades 7 & up).
~ Explains how to move on after painful abuse.

Pelzer, David. Lost Boy. Health Communications, 1997. (Grades 7 and up).
~ This true story about the author describes various foster homes and challenges that David faced after he was abused by his mother.

Prejudice/Racism

Desetta, Al, M.A. and Wolin, Sybil, Ph.D. <u>The Struggle to Be Strong True Stories by Teens About Overcoming Tough Times</u>. Free Spirit Publishing. (Grades 7 and up)
~ In 30 first-person accounts, teens tell how they overcame major life obstacles, including, drug abuse by loved ones, interracial relationships, abandonment, homosexuality, and more.

Griffin, John Howard. <u>Black Like Me</u>. Signet Book, 1996. (Grades 9 and up)
~ John Howard Griffin writes about his experiences as a white man who transforms himself with the aid of medication and dye in order to experience firsthand the life of a black man living in the Deep South in the 1950's.

Guy, Rosa and Binch, Caroline. <u>Billy the Great</u>. Doubleday, 1992. (Grades 3-6)
~ Billy teaches his parents a lesson about socioeconomic prejudices.

Houston, Julian. <u>New Boy</u>. Houghton Mifflin, 2005. (Grades 8-11)
~ The story of a fifteen year old boy who is the first to integrate a boarding school in Connecticut.

Hughes, Langston. <u>Not Without Laughter</u>. Touchstone Books, 1995. (Grades 8-12)
~ Depicts a Black family's attempts to deal with life in a small Kansas town.

Lee, Harper. <u>To Kill a Mockingbird</u>. Little Brown & Company, 1988. (Grades 8-12)
  ~ A lawyer's advice to his children as he defends the real mockingbird of Harper Lee's classic novel--a black man charged with the rape of a white girl. Through the young eyes of Scout and Jem Finch, Harper Lee explores the irrationality of adult attitudes toward race and class in the Deep South of the 1930s.

Masson, Sophie. <u>Sooner or Later</u>. University of Queensland Press,1991. (Grades 9-12)
  ~ When she comes to live with her father in a small Australian town, fifteen-year-old Scilla must deal with her shortcomings, with her grandmother's terminal illness, and with growing racial tensions.

Moloney, James. <u>Dougy</u>. University of Queensland Press, 1993. (Grades 9-12)
  ~ This novel gives the idea of the racist concern of Aborigines in Australia. When Dougy's sister, Gracey, is chosen for the State Athletics Championships, people in their small town were not all pleased. During the fight between the whites and blacks in the town, Dougy learns to be a leader for his family.

Muharrar, Aisha. <u>More Than a Label Why What You Wear or Who You're With Doesn't Define Who You Are.</u> Free Spirit Publishing. (Grades 6 – 12)
  ~ Written from the viewpoint of the 17-year-old author, various labels and how to deal with them are discussed. Also addressed are cliques, peer pressure, popularity, racism, sexism, and homophobia. This book empowers students and shows them how to assert their self-worth.

Myers, Walter Dean. <u>Hoops</u>. Laurel Leaf Books, 1981. (Grades 6-12)
  ~ Lonnie has to battle with the pressures of the ghetto while trying to go pro in basketball.

Neufeld, John. <u>Edgar Allan</u>. Puffin Books, 1999. (Grades 4-8)
  ~ A family adopts a young boy who is of a different race in the 1950's.

Parks, Gordon. <u>The Learning Tree</u>. Fawcett Books, 1987. (Grades 7 and up)
  ~ This is the story of a black family as they struggle to understand and accept the challenge of their special world.

Scoppetone, Sandra. <u>Happy Endings Are All Alike</u>. Alyson Publications, 2000. (Grades 9-12)

⁓ Small town prejudices emerge when a love affair between two teenage girls is revealed.

Sebestyen, Ouida. <u>Words By Heart</u>. New York: Little Brown, 1979. (Grades 6-8)
⁓ A young black girl struggles to fulfill her papa's dream of a better future for their family in the southwestern town where, in 1910, they are the only blacks.

Strasser, Todd and Rhue, Morton. <u>Wave</u>. Bantam Doubleday Dell Books for Young Readers, 1981. (Grades 7-12)
⁓ The powerful forces of group pressure that pervaded many historic movements such as Nazism are recreated in the classroom when history teacher Burt Ross introduces a "new" system to his students. And before long "The Wave," with its rules of "strength through discipline, community, and action," sweeps from the classroom through the entire school. And as most of the students join the movement, Laurie Saunders and David Collins recognize the frightening momentum of "The Wave" and realize they must stop it before it's too late.

Taylor, Theodore. <u>The Cay</u>. Yearling, 2002. (Grades 5 and up)
⁓ A white boy named Phillip has to survive on a small island with an old black man named Timothy. Phillip has to overcome his prejudices that deal with race and age.

Voigt, Cynthia. <u>Come a Stranger</u>. Simon Pulse, 1995. (Grades 7-12)
⁓ A young black girl named Mina has to overcome prejudices at a dance camp.

Voigt, Cynthia. <u>The Runner</u>. Scholastic, 1997. (Grades 7-12)
⁓ It was the 1960s, the time of the Vietnam War. "Bullet" Tillerman, the school track star, had to decide if he would go to fight or stay on the family farm. Bullet's father, who had already driven Bullet's older brother and sister out of the house, made impossible demands on him. And his mother seemed to have lost the will to resist the old man. Meanwhile, at school, a black student joined the track team, forcing Bullet to question his own prejudices.

Puberty

Bailey, Jacqui. <u>Sex, Puberty, and All That Stuff: A Guide to Growing Up</u>. Baron's Educational Series, Incorporated, 2004. (Grades 4-8)
- Girls and boys issues are addressed in separate chapters. Topics include: crushes, coping with controlling parents, menstruation, dating, and sexual activity, as well as how to survive the teen years.

Cole, Joanna. <u>Asking About Sex and Growing Up: A Question-and-Answer Book for Boys and Girls</u>. HarperCollins Publishers, 1998. (Grades 4-8)
- Written in a question-answer format, this book gets directly at the questions that many pre-teens have, but are afraid to ask about puberty and sexuality.

Fisher, Nick. <u>Living With a Willy</u>. Macmillan UK, 2004. (Grades 6-8)
- Designed to shed a light-hearted, but true perspective on what's going on down there for boys. Includes information on biological stages, real stories, image issues, shaving, tattooing, and girls.

Gravelle, Karen, and Leighton, Robert. <u>What's Going on Down There? Answers to Questions Boys Find Hard to Ask</u>. Walker and Company, 1998. (Grades 4-10)
- Along with answering the title question, sexual activity, homosexuality, and STDs are also addressed.

Jukes, Mavis. <u>Expecting the Unexpected</u>. Random House Children's Books, 1999. (Grades 4-8)

~ Twelve-year-old River gives readers a candid glimpse of what puberty and sex education are all about, including suspicions that her teenage sister is pregnant.

Kelly, Tara. <u>Dating and Relating: A Guy's Guide to Girls</u>. The Rosen Publishing Group, Incorporated, 1999. (Grades 6-8)
~ A guide for boys written by a girl. Topics include puberty, making friends with girls, flirting, how to kiss, reasons not to have sex, how to break up, and how to respect the opposite gender.

Le Jeune, Veronique, et. al. <u>Feeling Freakish? How to Be Comfortable in Your Own Skin</u>. Abrams, Harry N Inc., 2004. (Grades 6 and up)
~ Examines all aspects of puberty while focusing on a young adult's self-esteem in relation to all the changes going on in the body.

Madaras, Lynda and Madaras, Area. <u>The "What's Happening to My Body" Book for Girls</u>. Newmarket Press, 2007. (Grades 4-9)
~Addresses the body's changing size and shape, growth spurts, reproductive organs, the menstrual cycle, romantic and sexual feelings, puberty in girls and boys, and more.

O'Grady, Kathleen, ed. and Wansbrough, Paula, ed. <u>Sweet Secrets: Stories of Menstruation</u>. Second Story Press, 1997. (Grades 6-10)
~ This compilation of short stories puts menstruation in a positive light and tackles a variety of issues surrounding a young girl's first period.

Paulsen, Gary. <u>Amazing Life of Birds: The Nineteen-Day Puberty Journal of Duane Homer Leech</u>. Random House Children's Book, 2008. (Grades 6 and up)
~ Readers will identify with and take comfort in knowing that Duane has also gone through all the awkward changes.

Price, Geoffrey. <u>Puberty Boy</u>. Allen & Unwin Pty., Limited, 2006. (Grades 4-8)
~ This books provides reassuring information regarding: acne, sexual development, body odor, and other physical changes. The emotional changes in boys, as well as advice on how to interact with girls are also included. What makes this book great for boys is the real life stories from other boys and boys who've already grown up and gone through these changes.

Selzer, Adam.   How to Get Suspended and Influence People.   Random House Children's Books, 2007. (Grades 6 and up)
  ~ As an assignment for his gifted and talented class, Leon decides to "educate sixth and seventh graders" with a video on sex education. He started out in his smart-aleck, humorous ways, but began seeing his video as truly educational and comforting to those going through puberty. Soon, the whole town is in on this issue, as his video is censored out and he is suspended.

Springer, Nancy. Dussie. Walker & Company, 2007. (Grades 6-10)
  ~ Springer blends fictional mythology with one girls "catastrophic" venture through puberty.

Rape

Anderson, Kristen. The Truth about Sex by High School Senior Girls.
Kristen Anderson, 2000. (Grades 9 and up)
   ~ *The Truth about Sex by High School Senior Girls* was compiled using
quotes, insights, and statistics about sexual experiences from senior
girls. The book is pro-abstinence, based on the statistic that 74%
of the seniors regret sexual experiences they have had, and it takes
the view that sex is a beautiful and sacred rite to be shared in a fully
committed relationship. The book includes sections on older guys,
the first time, oral sex, STDs, pregnancy, sexual abuse and rape.

Anderson, Laurie Halse. Speak. Speak, 2001. (Grades 8-12)
   ~ What could have caused Melinda to suddenly fall mute? Could it
be due to the fact that no one at school is speaking to her because
she called the cops and got everyone busted at the seniors' big end-
of-summer party? Or maybe it's because her parents' only form of
communication is Post-It notes written on their way out the door
to their nine-to-whenever jobs. While Melinda is bothered by these
things, deep down she knows the real reason why she's been struck
mute: Andy Evans. He's a senior at Melinda's high school, and
Melinda hasn't been able to speak clearly since he raped her at the
senior party last August.

Baker, Keri. Once in a Green Room. Science & Humanities Press, 2001.
(Grades 10 and up)
   ~ After being raped and having an abortion while in college, a young
woman struggles to deal with her feelings and is ultimately helped by
the insights she gains from her special education students.

Bode, Janet. Rape: Preventing it; Coping with the Legal, Medical, and Emotional Aftermath. Watts, 1979. (Grades 9 and up)
    ~ Discusses the crime of rape: what it is, why it may occur, how to prevent it, and how to handle the legal, medical and emotional aftermath.

Chick, Sandra. Push Me Pull Me. Womens Pr Ltd, 1989. (Grades 9-12)
    ~ 14 year-old Cathy is raped by her mom's boyfriend. She washes and washes, but can't wash off the pain or guilt she feels. Then, very slowly, her anger surfaces and she begins to work it out.

Dessen, Sarah. Just Listen. Puffin, 2008. (Grades 9-12)
    ~ Annabel is being ostracized because of a supposed affair over the summer. What really happened was an attempted rape. In addition, Annabel's family has several troubles that they are denying.

Hyde, Margaret. Speak Out on Rape. McGraw, 1976. (Grades 7-12)
    ~ Provides information for those who want to prevent rape, help its victims, and break the stereotype of the rapist, including discussions on rape crisis centers, hotlines, and outdated laws and ways to change them.

Sparks, Beatrice. It Happened to Nancy. Avon, 1994. (Grades 9 and up)
    ~ A teenaged victim of AIDS recounts her battle with the disease in her diary, describing her first love, the night she was date-raped, her diagnosis of AIDS, and her thoughts and dreams.

Reform/making Positive Change

Crutcher, Chris. <u>Ironman</u>. HarperTeen, 2004. (Grades 8 and up)
~ Through an anger management class, troubled teens get to the root of what's troubling them and learn to make things better for themselves.

Hobbs, Will. <u>Downriver</u>. Bantam Doubleday Dell Books for Young Readers, 1996. (Grades 7 and up)
~ Fifteen-year-old Jessie and the other rebellious teenage members of a wilderness survival school team abandon their adult leader, hijack his boats, and try to run the dangerous white water at the bottom of the Grand Canyon.

Lipsyte, Robert. <u>The Contender</u>. HarperTrophy, 1987. (Grades 6-9)
~ Alfred is a high-school dropout working at a grocery store. His best friend is in a haze of drugs and violence, and now some street punks are harassing him for something he didn't do. Alfred gathers up the courage to visit Donatelli's Gym, the neighborhood's boxing club. He wants to be a champion--on the streets and in his own life.

Paulsen, Gary. <u>Alida's Song</u>. Yearling, 2001. (Grades 5-8)
~ A 14-year-old boy overcomes his parents' alcoholism and his own destructive and negative path when his grandmother invites him to work for the summer.

Thompson, Tate. <u>Senioritis</u>. May Davenport, 2003. (Grades 9 and up)
~ A group of high school teenagers have to attend a 3-5 p.m. program to make up credits, or to correct inappropriate behavior before they can graduate. A very compassionate mentor encourages them to

correct their failings as they vent their anger against teachers in their journals. The biggest strength of this novel is that low or high level readers can pick up this book and find at least one character who they know, or who they actually are.

Weill, Sabrina Solin. <u>We're Not Monsters: Teens Speak Out about Teens in Trouble.</u> HarperTempest, 2002. (Grades 8 – 12)
- Each chapter offers a variety of the issues including school shootings, anxiety, suicide, self-injury, and sex crimes, facts and statistics, plus advice and the voices of teenagers themselves. Weill also includes suggestions for further reading as well as phone numbers and Web addresses of organizations designed to help.

Wolff, Virginia Euwer.   <u>Make Lemonade</u>. Scholastic Paperbacks, 1994. (Grades 7-12)
- Two friends who are financially not well-off, show determination to succeed. One friend is the teenage mother of two and the other is determined to be the first in the family to go to college. This is a story that shows trials in life don't need to mean the end of dreams.

Relationships

Brashares, Ann. <u>Sisterhood of the Traveling Pants</u>. Dell Books for Young
    Readers, 2005. (Grades 7 and up)
    ~ The story of four very different friends who spend their summer
    apart. Each faces their own issues, but is comforted by the arrival
    of their thrift store jeans that magically fit everyone. Issues include
    having a friend with leukemia, relationship pressures, divorce, and
    family pressures.

Brashares, Ann. <u>Second Summer of the Sisterhood</u>. Dell Books for Young
    Readers, 2006. (Grades 8 and up)
    ~ Another summer is spent apart for the 4 friends. Again, each
    is comforted by the pair of thrift store jeans when they face issues
    such as: love lost and found, death, and finding the courage to live
    honestly.

Brashares, Ann. <u>Girls in Pants: The Third Summer of the Sisterhood</u>. Dell
    Books for Young Readers, 2007. (Grades 7 and up)
    ~ The third summer begins after the girls' high school graduation.
    The girls keep their ties close as they again face new issues. This
    time they face budding relationships, new step-siblings, tragedy in
    the family, and more heartbreak.

Brashares, Ann. <u>Forever in Blue: The Fourth Summer of the Sisterhood</u>.
    Delacorte Books for Young Readers, 2007. (Grades 8 and up)
    ~ This book takes a look at the girls' first take on college/post-high
    school life. Along with new opportunities come new issues: new
    love interests, loss of virginity, and breakups and makeups.

Courtney, Vicki. Teenvirtue 2: A Teen Girl's Guide to Relationships. B&H
   Publishing Group, 2006. (Grades 6-12)
   ~ Includes Christian advice for relationships including with friends,
   with boys, and with God.

Drew, Naomi, M.A. The Kids' Guide to Working Out Conflicts How
   to Keep Cool, Stay Safe, and Get Along. Free Spirit Publishing.
   (Grades 4-8)
   ~ Common forms of conflict, the reasons behind conflicts, and
   positive ways to deal with difficult circumstances are addressed.
   Self-tests and exercises are included to help young people discover
   whether they are conflict-solvers or conflict-makers. Drew also
   includes tips for bullying, calming down, lessening stress and
   tension, letting go of anger and resentment, and eliminating put-
   downs and other hurtful language.

Feig, Paul. Kick Me: Adventures in Adolescence. Three Rivers Press, 2002.
   (Grades 7-12).
   ~ Paul Feig takes you in a time machine to a world of bombardment
   by dodge balls, ill-fated prom dates, hellish school bus rides, and
   other aspects of public school life that will keep you laughing in
   recognition.

Fox, Annie M. Ed. Can You Relate? Real World Advice for Teens on Guys,
   Girls, Growing Up, and Getting Along. Free Spirit Publishing.
   ~ This book discusses teens' feelings, looks, and decisions, including
   relationships with boyfriends and girlfriends, authority figures,
   and friends. Also discussed is sex and sexuality; how to make a
   relationship work, and what to do when it doesn't.

Greenburg, Judith. Girl's Guide to Growing Up: Making the Right Choices.
   Scholastic Library Publishing, 2000. (Grades 5-8)
   ~ Addresses common issues faced in middle school, such as:
   relationships, temptations, self-image, risky behavior, and decisions
   middle school girls will be faced with.

Kelly, Tara. Dating and Relating: A Guy's Guide to Girls. The Rosen
   Publishing Group, Incorporated, 1999. (Grades 6-8)
   ~ A guide for boys written by a girl. Topics include puberty, making
   friends with girls, flirting, how to kiss, reasons not to have sex, how
   to break up, and how to respect the opposite gender.

McCoy, Kathy, and Wibbelsman, Charles, M.D. Life Happens: A Teenager's
   Guide to Friends, Failure, Sexuality, Love, Rejection, Addiction,

Peer Pressure, Families, Loss, Depression, Change, and Other challenges. Berkley Publishing, 1996. (Grades 7-12)
- Offers advice on how to cope with such feelings as sadness, anger, and anxiety related to various problems including the death of a family member, teen pregnancy, the end of a romantic relationship, being homosexual, and having an alcoholic parent.

Mortenson, Colin. A New Ladies' Man: Getting the Girl. Cambo Publishing, 2003. (Grades 9 and up).
- Advice for young men from someone who's been there. A humorous account that is meant to guide young gentlemen in the right direction.

Nelson, Blake. The New Rules of High School. Puffin, 2004. (Grades 9-12)
- An over-achieving senior breaks up with his long-time girlfriend and finds himself lost, but at the same time appreciating his normalcy.

Packer, Alex J., Ph.D. Bringing Up Parents The Teenager's Handbook. Free Spirit Press. (Grades 7-12).
- Includes suggestions on how teens can resolve conflicts with parents, improve family relationships, earn trust, accept responsibility, and help to create a healthier, happier home environment.

Packer, Alex J., Ph.D. The How Rude!™ Handbook of Friendship & Dating Manners for Teens Surviving the Social Scene. Free Spirit Publishing. (Grades 7 and up)
- Young adults learn how to have successful relationships.

Peterson, Jean Sunde. Talk with Teens about Feelings, Family, Relationships and the Future, Grades 7-12: 50 Guided Discussions for School and Counseling Groups. Free Spirit Publishing, Inc., 1997. (Grades 7-12)
- Fifty guided discussions on mood swings, anger, sadness, sexual behavior, violence, dating, career choices, and more help students share their feelings and   concerns and know they are not alone.

Williams, Carolyn Lynch. A Mother to Embarrass Me. Bantam Doubleday Books for Young Readers, 2003. (Grades 4-8)
- Many young people can empathize with Laura whose embarrassing mother yodels and walks around in clay-covered pajamas. To make matters worse, Laura's mother just announced that she's pregnant.

Religion

Carlson, Melody. <u>Becoming Me: Diary of a Teenage Girl, Book 1</u>. Multnomah, 2000. (Grades 8-10)
- The story of a Christian girl's transition from childhood to womanhood. Issues addressed include: peer pressure, loyalty, conflict with parents, the longing for a boyfriend, and her own spirituality.

Courtney, Vicky. <u>Teenvirtue: Real Issues, Real Life. . . A Teen Girl's Survival Guide</u>. B&H Publishing Group, 2005. (Grades 6-12)
- Offers Christian advice for issues such as: friendships, boys, fashion and beauty, and heavier issues such as Internet safety, sex and drugs. The format is not "preachy," but resembles that of popular magazines.

Courtney, Vicki. <u>Teenvirtue 2: A Teen Girl's Guide to Relationships</u>. B&H Publishing Group, 2006. (Grades 6-12)
- Includes Christian advice for relationships including with friends, with boys, and with God.

Rainey, Dennis and Rainey, Barbara. <u>So You're About to be a Teenager: Godly Advice for Preteens</u>. Thomas Nelson, 2003. (Grades 6-9)
- A preview of what teens may be faced with and Christian guidance with how to deal with those issues.

Sandell, Lisa Ann. <u>The Weight of the Sky</u>. Viking Juvenile, 2006. (Grades 8 and up)
- Sarah is harassed because she is the only Jewish student in her high school class. She learns to embrace her religion when she travels to Israel.

Youngs, Bettie B. <u>Living the Ten Commandments in New Times: A Book for Teens</u>. Faith Communications, 2004. (Grades 8 and up)
- The Ten Commandments are reviewed and related to teens today. It dispels the myth that the ten commandments are no longer meaningful.

Risky Behaviors

Bleich, Alan Ralph. <u>Coping With Health Risks and Risky Behavior</u>. The Rosen Publishing Group, Incorporated, 1990.
~ Addresses numerous health risks including sexual behavior, smoking, drinking, drugs, and psychological problems.

Greenburg, Judith. <u>Girl's Guide to Growing Up: Making the Right Choices</u>. Scholastic Library Publishing, 2000. (Grades 5-8)
~ Addresses common issues faced in middle school, such as: relationships, temptations, self-image, risky behavior, and decisions middle school girls will be faced with.

Rebman, Renee. <u>Addictions and Risky Behaviors: Cutting, Bingeing, Snorting, and Other Risky Behaviors</u>. Enslow Publishers, Incorporated, 2006.
~The causes and signs of these addictions are addressed by Rebman. Also addressed is how those who are addicted can be helped.

Runaway/Kidnap

Bawden, Nina. <u>The Finding</u>. Lothrop, 1985. (Grades 5-8)
    ~ Alex runs away from his adoptive family during a crisis, but returns at the end of the crisis.

Conroy, Frank. <u>Stop-Time</u>. Penguin Books, 1993. (Grades 9-12)
    ~ This is an autobiography that is a memoir of boyhood and adolescence. Beginning with a lesson in brutality at a progressive boarding school, the book moves to a self-help settlement in Florida, a Connecticut mental hospital (where Conroy's mother and stepfather are wardens), and to New York City (where he survives by his wits in schools, at jobs, and even more dangerously at home). Then, after his mother leaves for Europe and his stepfather installs an insane mistress in the family's apartment, Conroy runs away, embarking on new adventures.

Ehrlich, Amy. <u>Where it Stops, Nobody Knows</u>. Puffin Books, 1990. (Grades 9-12)
    ~ Nina has always moved around a lot. It's not until Junior High that she realizes her "mother" is on the run because she actually kidnapped Nina as a baby.

Hale, Erica. <u>Catch the Sun.</u> Rainbow Publishing, 1987. (Grades 9-12)
    ~ Fed up with her drunken stepfather and her dead end job, Lennie runs away.

Johnson, Joan. <u>Kids Without Homes</u>. Scholastic Library, 1991. (Grades 9 and up)

- Examines homelessness in today's society as it affects our nation's youth, their education, upbringing, opportunities for employment, involovement with crime, and prospects for fixing their situation.

Stewart, Bridgett and White, Franklin. <u>No Matter What</u>. Blue/Black Press, 2002. (Grades 7-12)
- Bridgett Stewart shares her journey through unthinkable poverty and discusses everything from gaining her own self-respect when no one else would respect her because of where she lived to surviving verbal abuse from classmates, living without a father, school pressures, and her decision to use education as a vehicle from poverty while earning a 4.0 grade point average in tough and trying times. Stewart also discusses self-esteem, alcohol and drugs, and many other topics.

Self-Inflicted Pressure

Adderholdt, Miriam, Ph.D. and Goldberg, Jan. <u>Perfectionism: What's Bad About Being Too Good?</u> (Revised and Updated Edition). Free Spirit Publishing. (Grades 7-12).
  ⁓ Explains the differences between healthy ambition and unhealthy perfectionism and gives strategies for getting out of the perfectionism trap—from recognizing the symptoms to rewarding yourself for who you are, not what you do.

Barry, Douglas. <u>Wisdom for a Young Ceo: Incredible Letters and Inspiring Advice from Today's Business Leaders</u>. Running Press Book Publishers, 2004 . (Grades 8 and up)
  ⁓ At 14 years old, Douglas Barry wrote to numerous CEOs for advice on climbing to the top. This book highlights the responses and his research.

Elkind, David. <u>All Grown Up and No Place to Go: Teenagers in Crisis</u>. Perseus Books Group, 1997. (Grades 9 and up)
  ⁓ Elkind makes a case for protecting teens instead of pressuring them. This book addresses long work hours, rising violence, and pregnancies.

Greenspon, Thomas S., Ph.D. <u>Freeing Our Families from Perfectionism</u>. Free Spirit Publishing. (Grades 9 and up).
  ⁓ Tom Greenspon explains perfectionism, where it comes from, and what to do about it. Readers will learn how to change perfectionism into self-acceptance.

Guy, David. <u>Football Dreams</u>. Penguin Books, 1980. (Grades 6-12)

~ A teenager struggles through a private academy in order to live up to his father's dreams for the future. Through his experience, he learns that winning isn't everything.

Kerr, M.E. <u>If I Loved You, Am I Trapped Forever</u>? Harper and Row, 1982. (Grades 6-12)
~ Allan Bennett has a lot of pressure and expectations. He has much to contend with in preserving his image.

Nelson, Blake. <u>The New Rules of High School</u>. Puffin, 2004. (Grades 9-12)
~ An over-achieving senior breaks up with his long-time girlfriend and finds himself lost, but at the same time appreciating his normalcy.

Rostkowski, Margaret. <u>The Best of Friends</u>. Harper and Row, 1989. (Grades 9-12)
~ Dan, a bright perfectionist driven by his demanding father, teaches that perfectionism is a serious problem.

Sparks, Beatrice. <u>Kim: Empty Inside: The Diary of an Anonymous Teenager</u>. Avon Books, 2002. (Grades 7-10)
~ Seventeen-year-old Kim, feeling the pressure of maintaining an A average to stay on her college gymnastics team, becomes obsessive about her weight and develops anorexia.

Stewart, Bridgett and White, Franklin. <u>No Matter What</u>. Blue/Black Press, 2002. (Grades 7-12)
~ Bridgett Stewart shares her journey through unthinkable poverty and discusses everything from gaining her own self-respect when no one else would respect her because of where she lived to surviving verbal abuse from classmates, living without a father, school pressures, and her decision to use education as a vehicle from poverty while earning a 4.0 grade point average in tough and trying times. Stewart also discusses self-esteem, alcohol and drugs, and many other topics.

Tashijan, Janet. <u>Multiple Choice</u>. Henry Holt & Company, Incorporated, 1999. (Grades 8 and up)
~ For as long as Monica Devon can remember, she has been two things: a whiz at making anagrams and a perfectionist who obsesses about saying and doing the right thing. Seeing no other way out from her compulsive nature, she creates "Multiple Choice," a roulette word game that will force spontaneity into her life. At first the game is exciting, but soon it gets dangerous. Fortunately for Monica, help is closer than she thinks.

Thompson, Julian. <u>Simon Pure</u>. Scholastic Books, 1987. (Grades 9-12)
    - Simon Storm is a gifted fifteen year old college freshman who must deal with the pressures of college.

Yee, Lisa. <u>Millicent Min, Girl Genius</u>. Arthur A. Levine, 2003. (Grades 5-8)
    - Millicent Min is about a 12 year old girl in the 11th grade. She is really smart and wants to spend her summer reading and taking a college class. Her mom signs her up for volleyball and she's not accepted by the other kids. In order to keep a new friend, she lies about her intelligence and all of her accomplishments.

Yoo, Paula. <u>Good Enough</u>. HarperTeen, 2008. (Grades 8-12)
    - Patti is working really hard to impress her parents. Along the way she discovers there's more to life, and begins to work hard to fit in with everyone else in her class.

Self-Esteem

American Association of University Women, Haag, Pamela Susan. <u>Voices of a Generation: Teenage Girls on Sex, School and Self.</u> Avalon Publishing Group, 2001. (Grades 7-12)
- <u>Voices of a Generation</u> draws on the responses of more than 2,000 girls ages 12 to 16 who participated in day long "Sister-to-Sister" summits held in 50 locations nationwide in 1998. Girls were asked to identify the major issues and struggles in their lives, to speculate on how their schools could help them, and to talk about what they would like to tell other girls - and what they would like to know from other girls - among other themes.

Armstrong, Thomas, Ph.D. <u>You're Smarter Than You Think - A Kid's Guide to Multiple Intelligences.</u> Free Spirit Publishing. (Grades 7-12).
- Explains the eight intelligences, and describes ways to develop each one. Armstrong demonstrates how to use all eight intelligences in school, build them at home, and how to use them in the future.

Cleary, Beverly. <u>Jean and Johnny.</u> HarperTrophy, 1996. (Grades 5-8)
- A story about a girl who lacks self-confidence and a boy who has too much.

Dayton, Tian. <u>It's My Life! A Workout for Your Mind</u>. Health Communications, Incorporated, 2000. (Grades 5-12)
- The teenage years are transition years, when children move from childhood into adulthood. It is an often-turbulent time, marked by constant change, transformation and, frequently, confusion. In this hand-on Dayton guides teens on the journey of self-exploration. She

explains that the most important relationship we will ever develop and have in our lives is with ourselves. When we get to know ourselves and accept our own internal feelings and motivations and work with instead of run from them, we can become stronger and healthier people. Exercises are designed to help teens express their feelings or to look at them from a fresh perspective.

Fox, Annie M. Ed. <u>Can You Relate? Real World Advice for Teens on Guys, Girls, Growing Up, and Getting Along.</u> Free Spirit Publishing.
~ This book discusses teens' feelings, looks, and decisions, including relationships with boyfriends and girlfriends, authority figures, and friends. Also discussed is sex and sexuality; how to make a relationship work, and what to do when it doesn't.

Fredericks, Mariah. <u>The True Meaning of Cleavage</u>. Simon & Schuster Children's, 2004.
~ Frederick's portrays one ninth-grader's struggle with her friend becoming "the other girl." When Jess and Sari enter high school, the two buds fully expect the usual popularity contests that divide the "in" kids from the "out." This is a novel that helps teen readers take stock of their own pride and dignity (*Shana Taylor*).

Gallo, Donald R. <u>On the Fringe</u>. Puffin, 2003. (Grades 6 and up)
~ In every school at every grade, there's a pecking order among students-an in crowd and those outside it, who are often ridiculed mercilessly for the "crime" of being different. A tomboy finds the relief of self-expression through her music, while in another tale a relentless bully tests the faith of an intensely religious girl. A cheerleader discovers that the true soul of her school can't be found within the cool clique; a football player finally stands up for a harassed fellow student; and a boy watches in horror as the school "freak" marches into his classroom with a loaded rifle.

Kaufman, Gershen, Raphael, Lev, and Espeland, Pamela. <u>Stick up for Yourself : Every Kid's Guide to Personal Power & Positive Self-Esteem</u>. Free Spirit Publishing, 2000.(Grades 6-10)
~A self-help guide to positive thinking, high self-esteem, and responsible personal power. The book's premise is that all young people can and should be taught the skills necessary to face common issues, such as making choices, liking themselves, and solving problems. Exercises guide readers through learning about their own feelings, dreams, and needs--while stressing that they are responsible for their own behavior and happiness.

Kirberger, Kimberly. <u>No Body's Perfect</u>. Scholastic, Inc., 2003. (Grades 6 and up)
  ~ Why bother learning to accept, appreciate, and love your body just the way it is? Because it's a part of you, and when you love yourself, you love every part of yourself, even the parts that aren't "perfect." Accepting yourself just the way you are may seem like a pretty big challenge. It may even seem impossible. But it's not.

Le Jeune, Veronique, et. al. <u>Feeling Freakish? How to Be Comfortable in Your Own Skin</u>. Abrams, Harry N Inc., 2004. (Grades 6 and up)
  ~ Examines all aspects of puberty while focusing on a young adult's self-esteem in relation to all the changes going on in the body.

Orenstein, Peggy. <u>SchoolGirls: Young Women, Self-Esteem, and the Confidence Gap</u>. Knopf Publishing Group, 1995. (Grades 7-12)
  ~ In 1990, the AAUW conducted a poll that highlighted how young girls lose their self-esteem as they reach adolescence. They emerge from adolescence with reduced expectations of life, and much less confidence in themselves and their abilities than boys have.

Palardy, Debra J. <u>Sweetie Here's the Best Reason on the Planet to Say No to Your Boyfriend: Even If You've Already Said Yes</u>. Dorrance Pub Co, 2000. (Grades 8 and up)
  ~ This book is for adolescents who may have felt pressured to engage in activities in which they were not always comfortable or completely willing. It addresses the issue of changing morals in schools and concerns that this may be enough to make even the most straight-laced young lady feel that sexual activity is okay. Author Debra J. Palardy presents a collection of lines used by hormone-driven teenage boys to get their girlfriends to engage in sex. She follows through and provides useful comeback and advice for girls, considering their boyfriends' pleas. The author provides the objective wisdom sought by teenagers too embarrassed, timid, or afraid to consult those closet to them. Her guide points out the pitfalls of becoming sexually active, including pregnancy, sexually transmitted disease, and loss of self-esteem. She urges teenage girls to seek guidance from women who have had the time to develop an adult perspective and look back on their own experiences.

Peterson, Jean Sunde. <u>Talk with Teens about Feelings, Family, Relationships and the Future, Grades 7-12: 50 Guided Discussions for School and Counseling Groups</u>. Free Spirit Publishing, Inc., 1997. (Grades 7-12)

- Fifty guided discussions on mood swings, anger, sadness, sexual behavior, violence, dating, career choices, and more help students share their feelings and concerns and know they are not alone.

Romain, Trevor and Verdick, Elizabeth. <u>Bullies Are a Pain in the Brain.</u> Free Spirit Publishing, 1997. (Grades 6-8)
- Every child needs to know how to cope with bullies, and this book blends humor with serious, practical suggestions that will help kids understand, avoid and stand up to bullies while preserving their own self-esteem.

Simmons, Rachel. <u>Odd Girl Out: The Hidden Culture of Aggression in Girls.</u> Harcourt Brace & Company, 2003. (Grades 9 and up)
- Why are girls becoming more aggressive in their everyday lives, and how is it affecting their overall self-esteem? Rachel Simmons, a Rhodes scholar who has painstakingly researched female bullying and the psychology of girls, feels that girls' aggressiveness is just as harmful as that of boys but is much harder to recognize..

Stewart, Bridgett and White, Franklin. <u>No Matter What</u>. Blue/Black Press, 2002. (Grades 7-12)
- Bridgett Stewart shares her journey through unthinkable poverty and discusses everything from gaining her own self-respect when no one else would respect her because of where she lived to surviving verbal abuse from classmates, living without a father, school pressures, and her decision to use education as a vehicle from poverty while earning a 4.0 grade point average in tough and trying times. Stewart also discusses self-esteem, alcohol and drugs, and many other topics.

Westerfield, Scott. <u>Uglies</u>. Simon and Schuster, 2006. (Grades 6 and up)
- Young girls start to question the idea of everyone being ugly until they turn 16, when they'll undergo an operation to conform and be made "pretty" by their society's standards.

Westerfield, Scott. <u>Pretties</u>. Simon and Schuster, 2006. (Grades 6 and up)
- Tally struggles to overcome her transformation from an "Ugly" to a "Pretty." She strives to remember what it was like to have an individuality.

Self-Mutilation

Alderman, Tracy. The Scarred Soul: Understanding & Ending Self-Inflicted Violence. New Harbinger Publications, 1997. (Grades 9 and up)
- Written for the victims of this addiction--and for mental health professionals—*The Scarred Soul* explores the reasons behind this behavior and shows how to overcome the psychological traps that lead to self-destructive acts.

Levenkron, Steven. Cutting: Understanding and Overcoming Self-Mutilation. W. W. Norton & Company, 1999. (Grades 9 and up)
- The author explains the phenomena of self-mutilation, a disorder that affects as many as two million Americans. Cutting takes the reader through the psychological experience of the person who seeks relief from mental pain and anguish in self-inflicted physical pain. Steven Levenkron traces the components that predispose a personality to becoming a self-mutilator: genetics, family experience, childhood trauma, and parental behavior. Written for the self-mutilator, parents, friends, and therapists, Levenkron explains why the disorder manifests in self-harming behaviors and, most of all, describes how the self- mutilator can be helped.

McKormick, Patricia. Cut. Push, 2002. (Grades 7-12)
- This novel deals with mental illness. Teens will relate to the adolescent drama and all-important friends as the main character tries to "cut" it. Its readers will find hope in the uplifting end.

Rebman, Renee. Addictions and Risky Behaviors: Cutting, Bingeing, Snorting, and Other Risky Behaviors. Enslow Publishers, Incorporated, 2006.
~The causes and signs of these addictions are addressed by Rebman. Also addressed is how those who are addicted can be helped.

Strong, Marilee. A Bright Red Scream: Self-Mutilation and the Language of Pain. Penguin Books, 1999. (Grades 9 and up)
~ An award-winning journalist explores one of today's most misunderstood phenomena--self-mutilation. Self-mutilation is a behavior so shocking that it is almost never discussed. Yet estimates are that upwards of eight million Americans are chronic self-injurers. They are people who use knives, razor blades, or broken glass to cut themselves. Their numbers include the actor Johnny Depp and *Girl Interrupted* author Susanna Kaysen.

Diana. Weill, Sabrina Solin. We're Not Monsters: Teens Speak Out about Teens in Trouble. HarperTempest, 2002. (Grades 8 – 12)
~ Each chapter offers a variety of the issues including school shootings, anxiety, suicide, self-injury, and sex crimes, facts and statistics, plus advice and the voices of teenagers themselves. Weill also includes suggestions for further reading as well as phone numbers and Web addresses of organizations designed to help.

Sexual Abuse

Anderson, Kristen. The Truth about Sex by High School Senior Girls.
Kristen Anderson, 2002. (Grades 9 and up)
~ *The Truth about Sex by High School Senior Girls* was compiled
using quotes, insights, and statistics about sexual experiences from
senior girls. The book is pro-abstinence, based on the statistic that
74% of the seniors regret sexual experiences they have had, and it
takes the view that sex is a beautiful and sacred rite to be shared
in a fully committed relationship. The book includes sections on
older guys, the first time, oral sex, STDs, pregnancy, sexual abuse
and rape.

Anderson, Laurie Halse. Speak. Speak, 2001. (Grades 9 and up)
Melinda had no chance of "making it" socially when she called the
cops on a party the summer before her freshman year. Because of
this, she is afraid to "speak" about what really happened until her
friend starts dating her nightmare.

Bass, Ellen. I Never Told Anyone: Writings by Women Survivors of Child
Sexual Abuse. Perennial, 1991. (Grades 9 and up)
~ Stories from the survivors of childhood sexual abuse offer accounts
of women struggling to come to terms with their emotional response
to abuse. It reassures the reader that she is not alone.

Bass, Ellen. The Courage to Heal. Perennial, 1994. (Grades 9 and up)
~ An inspiring, comprehensive guide that offers hope and
encouragement to every woman who was sexually abused as a child
-- and those who care about her.

Blume, E. Sue. <u>Secret Survivors</u>. Ballantine Books, 1991. (Grades 9 and up)
~ A reassuring guide to survivors of incest.

Crutcher, Chris. <u>Chinese Handcuffs</u>. Laurel Leaf, 1991. (Grades 9-12)
~ When Dillon Hemingway is forced to witness his brother Preston's suicide, his life understandably seems to fall apart. His quest to make it whole again involves Stacy Ryder, Preston's girlfriend, who is left with more than a memory of Dillon's dead brother, and Jennifer Lawless, a star high school basketball player with a secret too monstrous to tell and too enormous to keep.

Feuereisen, Patti. <u>Invisible Girls: The Truth About Sexual Abuse.</u> Seal Press, 2005. (Grades 9 and up).
~ The following issues are addressed: female sexuality and abuse, contributing family dynamics, advice on preventing, reporting, and recovering from abuse, father-daughter incest, other incest, abuse by teachers and clergy, and different types of rape. It provides hope that healing is possible.

Frost, Helen. <u>Keesha's House</u>. Farrar, Straus, and Giroux, 2003. (Grades 9 and up)
~ Joe's mother died when he was young. His aunt took him in when he was 12, and he now owns that house. Keesha's dad is a mean drunk so Joe takes her in. Also in the book is a pregnant 16 year old, a young man whose father threw him out because he is gay, a victim of sexual abuse, a child who's been abandoned then ends up in juvie, a child whose parents are in jail.

Kellogg, Majorie. <u>Like the Lion's Tooth</u>. Farrar, Straus, and Giroux, 1972. (Grades 5-9)
~ Eleven year old Ben, who has been physically and sexually abused by his father, is sent to school for "problem children." Ben eventually resigns himself to the situation.

Lowery, Linda. <u>Laurie Tells</u>. Carolrhoda, 1993. (Grades 8 and up)
~ Laurie, unable to get help from her mother for her father's molestation, is finally helped by an aunt. The story is told in Laurie's words.

Miklowitz, Gloria. <u>Secrets Not Meant to Be Kept</u>. Laurel-Leaf Books, 1989. (Grades 9-12)
~ Teenager Adrienne Meyer doesn't understand why she can't be more intimate with her boyfriend, Ryan until she discovers that she, her sister, and countless other children were sexually abused by the preschool staff 12 years ago.

Pledge, Deanna S., Ph.D. <u>When Something Feels Wrong A Survival Guide About Abuse for Young People.</u> Free Spirit Publishing. (Grades 7 and up)

~ *When Something Feels Wrong* reassures young adults with a history of being abused (physically, emotionally, or sexually). Pledge includes checklists and journaling ideas to help readers to explore their feelings and experiences. There are also real life examples to show readers they're not alone.

Wachter, Oralee. <u>Close to Home</u>. Scholastic, 1986. (Grades 8 and up)

~ Four short stories on the theme of child molestation describe some dangerous situations and how to deal with them.

Wachter, Oralee. <u>No More Secrets for Me</u>. Little Brown, 1983. (Grades 6 and up)

~ Sexual abuse and dangerous situations are discussed, as well as the fact that the abuser is often someone close to the child.

Weill, Sabrina Solin. <u>We're Not Monsters: Teens Speak Out about Teens in Trouble.</u> HarperTempest, 2002. (Grades 8 – 12)

~ Each chapter offers a variety of issues including school shootings, anxiety, suicide, self-injury, and sex crimes, facts and statistics, plus advice and the voices of teenagers themselves. Weill also includes suggestions for further reading as well as phone numbers and Web addresses of organizations designed to help.

Sexuality, Teenage

Alexander, Ruth Bell. <u>Changing Bodies, Changing Lives: A Book for Teens on Sex and Relationships</u>. Three Rivers Press, 1998. (Grades 8 and up)

  - *Changing Bodies, Changing Lives* has helped teenagers make informed decisions about their lives, from questions about sex, love, friendship, and how your body works to dealing with problems at school and home and figuring out who you are.

Anderson, Kristen. <u>The Truth about Sex by High School Senior Girls</u>. Kristen Anderson, 2003. (Grades 9 and up)

  - *The Truth about Sex by High School Senior Girls* was compiled using quotes, insights, and statistics about sexual experiences from senior girls. The book is pro-abstinence, based on the statistic that 74% of the seniors regret sexual experiences they have had, and it takes the view that sex is a beautiful and sacred rite to be shared in a fully committed relationship. The book includes sections on older guys, the first time, oral sex, STDs, pregnancy, sexual abuse and rape.

Basso, Michael J. <u>The Underground Guide to Teenage Sexuality: An Essential Handbook for Today's Teens and Parents</u>. Fairview, 2003. (Grades 9 and up)

  - A guide to teen sexuality—updated and expanded with information on sexually-transmitted diseases; contraception; sexual abuse, healthy relationships; hotlines and resources; and much more.

Bell, Ruth. <u>Changing Bodies, Changing Lives: A Book for Teens on Sex and Relationships.</u> Vintage Books USA, 1988. (Grades 8 and up)
~ Addresses the need for open dialogue between teenagers on the topics of sex and relationships. Informs them on how to prevent unwanted pregnancies and sexually transmitted diseases. Updated to include material on suicide, AIDS and food and drug abuse.

Bode, Janet, and Mack, Stan. <u>Heartbreak and Roses: Real Life Stories of Troubled Love.</u> Franklin Watts, 2000. (Grades 8 and up)
~ Teens from around the United States reflect on love, sexual behavior, and relationships with their parents and friends.

Carey, Joely. <u>Boys and Sex.</u> Barron's Educational Series, 2002. (Grades 8 and up)
~ This book tells every girl what they should know about boys, and what boys really want from girls. The author advises girls on how to deal with emerging sexual emotions and how to say no to unwanted sex. She also explains the physical facts of sex and the use of contraceptives, and advises on what to do if pregnancy occurs. Titles in this series are frank guides intended to help teenage girls deal with the many uncertainties and challenges that are a part of growing up.

Courtney, Vicky. <u>Teenvirtue: Real Issues, Real Life. . . A Teen Girl's Survival Guide</u>. B&H Publishing Group, 2005. (Grades 6-12)
~ Offers Christian advice for issues such as: friendships, boys, fashion and beauty, and heavier issues such as Internet safety, sex and drugs. The format is not "preachy," but resembles that of popular magazines.

Courtney, Vicki. <u>Teenvirtue 2: A Teen Girl's Guide to Relationships</u>. B&H Publishing Group, 2006. (Grades 6-12)
~ Includes Christian advice for relationships including with friends, with boys, and with God.

Daldry, Jeremy. <u>The Teenage Guy's Survival Guide : The Real Deal on Girls, Growing Up and Other Guy Stuff.</u> Megan Tingley, 1999. (Grades 7 and up)
~ A humorous guide for boys, offering advice on dating, sex, body changes, and social life.

Fox, Annie M. Ed. <u>Can You Relate? Real World Advice for Teens on Guys, Girls, Growing Up, and Getting Along.</u> Free Spirit Publishing.

~ This book discusses teens' feelings, looks, and decisions, including relationships with boyfriends and girlfriends, authority figures, and friends. Also discussed is sex and sexuality; how to make a relationship work, and what to do when it doesn't.

Garden, Nancy. The Year They Burned Books. Farrar, Strauss, and Giroux, 1999. (Grades 9-12).
~ Controversy begins with an open editorial in the school newspaper, condoning the distribution of condoms. Jamie's realization that she's gay adds to the issues addressed in this book.

Gravelle, Karen, et al. What's Going on Down There: Answers to Questions Boys Find Hard to Ask. Walker & Company, 1998. (Grades 9 and up)
~ Describes the physical and emotional changes that occur in boys (and, to a lesser extent, in girls) during puberty and discusses sexual activity, homosexuality, AIDS, and other related topics.

Hatchell, Deborah. What Smart Teenagers Know...About Dating, Relationships & Sex. Piper Books, 2003. (Grades 9 and up)
~ Hatchell's book includes real-life stories by teenagers. It's also a hands-on guide that teens (both boys and girls) can use, starting immediately.

Kelly, Tara. Dating and Relating: A Guy's Guide to Girls. The Rosen Publishing Group, Incorporated, 1999. (Grades 6-8)
~ A guide for boys written by a girl. Topics include puberty, making friends with girls, flirting, how to kiss, reasons not to have sex, how to break up, and how to respect the opposite gender.

Lerman, Evelyn. Teen Moms: The Pain and the Promise. Morning Glory, 1997. (Grades 10 and up)
~ The text represents two years of interviews with 50 teens who were either pregnant or had children. She explores why teens have sex, young women's experiences with men, and what motherhood means to these young mothers. Issues about public assistance and independence and even an exploration of the positive effects of teen pregnancy are explored. The last chapter is for adults who want to have a positive impact on the lives of young adults.

Palardy, Debra J. Sweetie Here's the Best Reason on the Planet to Say No to Your Boyfriend: Even If You've Already Said Yes. Dorrance Pub Co, 2000. (Grades 8 and up)
~ This book is for adolescents who may have felt pressured to engage in activities in which they were not always comfortable or completely

willing. It addresses the issue of changing morals in schools and concerns that this may be enough to make even the most straight-laced young lady feel that sexual activity is okay. Author Debra J. Palardy presents a collection of lines used by hormone-driven teenage boys to get their girlfriends to engage in sex. She follows through and provides useful comeback and advice for girls, considering their boyfriends' pleas. The author provides the objective wisdom sought by teenagers too embarrassed, timid, or afraid to consult those closet to them. Her guide points out the pitfalls of becoming sexually active, including pregnancy, sexually transmitted disease, and loss of self-esteem. She urges teenage girls to seek guidance from women who have had the time to develop an adult perspective and look back on their own experiences.

Peterson, Jean Sunde. Talk with Teens about Feelings, Family, Relationships and the Future: 50 Guided Discussions for School and Counseling Groups. Free Spirit Publishing, Inc., 1997. (Grades 7-12)
- Fifty guided discussions on mood swings, anger, sadness, sexual behavior, violence, dating, career choices, and more help students share their feelings and concerns and know they are not alone.

Ponton, Lynn, MD. The Sex Lives of Teenagers: Revealing the Secret World of Adolescent Boys and Girls. Plume Books, 2001. (Grades 9 and up)
- With more and more teenagers having sex by the age of sixteen and others feeling pressured to before they're ready, parents and adolescents must find ways to communicate openly and honestly about a subject that has been ignored for too long. Lynn Ponton, M.D., takes a look at what teenagers have to say about their sexual lives. In a safe forum, without fear of judgment or censorship, teens feel free to speak frankly about their feelings, desires, fantasies, and expectations. And parents give voice to the struggle of coming to terms with their children's emerging sexual identities. Dr. Ponton opens a dialogue that addresses controversial topics such as pregnancy, abortion, masturbation, sexual orientation, Internet dating, and gender roles. Sensitive subjects such as AIDS and drugs are also explored.

Rainey, Dennis, Barbara, Samuel, and Rebecca. So You're About to Be a Teenager: Godly Advice for Preteens on Friends, Love, Sex, Faith and Other Life Issues. Nelson Books, 2003. (Grades 6 and up)
- Samuel and Rebecca Rainey share their perspective as young adults who recall their own successes and failures as teenagers. They cover

the topics of friends, peer pressure, boundaries, dating, and sex. The Raineys address the most common traps of adolescence and teach young people how to avoid making poor choices.

Scott, Sharon. <u>How to Say No and Keep Your Friends: Peer Pressure Reversal for Teens and Preteens</u>. Human Resource Development Press, 1997. (Grades 5-12)

    ~ This book presents teens/preteens with very specific ways to manage all kinds of negative peer pressure--from gossip and cliques to the most serious problem invitations including drugs, sex, and even violence.

Swisher, Karin L., Leone, Bruno, and O'Neil, Terry. <u>Teenage Sexuality: Opposing Viewpoints</u>. Gale Group, 1994. (Grades 9 and up)

    ~ An examination of birth control, sex education, STDs, homosexuality, pregnancy, and changes in the attitudes toward teenage sexuality and morality. The book explores a wide range of opinions and perspectives. *(Doris A. Fong)*

Sexually Transmitted Diseases (STDs)

Anderson, Kristen. <u>The Truth about Sex by High School Senior Girls</u>. Kristen Anderson, 2004.(Grades 9 and up)

  ~ *The Truth about Sex by High School Senior Girls* was compiled using quotes, insights, and statistics about sexual experiences from senior girls. The book is pro-abstinence, based on the statistic that 74% of the seniors regret sexual experiences they have had, and it takes the view that sex is a beautiful and sacred rite to be shared in a fully committed relationship. The book includes sections on older guys, the first time, oral sex, STDs, pregnancy, sexual abuse and rape.

Basso, Michael J. <u>The Underground Guide to Teenage Sexuality</u>. Fairview Press, 2003. (Grades 9 and up)

  ~ Presents facts about human sexuality, including anatomy, sexually transmitted diseases, contraception, homosexuality, and sexual intercourse.

Bell, Ruth. <u>Changing Bodies, Changing Lives: A Book for Teens on Sex and Relationships.</u> Vintage Books USA, 1988. (Grades 8 and up)

  ~ Addresses the need for open dialogue between teenagers on the topics of sex and relationships. Informs them on how to prevent unwanted pregnancies and sexually transmitted diseases. Updated to include material on suicide, AIDS and food and drug abuse.

Curran, Christine Perdan. <u>Sexually Transmitted Diseases</u>. Enslow Publishers, Incorporated, 1998. (Grades 8 and up)

‑ Examines the history, symptoms, treatment, and prevention of such sexually transmitted diseases as syphilis, gonorrhea, herpes, AIDS, and hepatitis.

Swisher, Karin L., Leone, Bruno, and O'Neil, Terry. <u>Teenage Sexuality: Opposing Viewpoints</u>. Gale Group, 1994. (Grades 9 and up)
‑ An examination of birth control, sex education, STDs, homosexuality, pregnancy, and changes in the attitudes toward teenage sexuality and morality. The book explores a wide range of opinions and perspectives. *(Doris A. Fong)*

Sibling Rivalry

Amadeo, D.M. There's a Little Bit of Me in Jamey. Whitman & Co, 1989. (Grades 5-8)
- Brian, whose younger brother Jamey has leukemia, feels frightened, confused, and neglected by his parents; but he finds some comfort when he donates bone marrow to his brother.

Byers, Betsy. The Summer of the Swans. Viking, 1970. (Grades 4-8)
- A teen-aged girl gains insight into her priorities when her mentally challenged brother becomes lost.

Gehert, Jeanne. I'm Somebody Too. Verbal Images Press, 1992. (Grades 5-8)
- Emily, 12, has a younger brother who is hyperactive and a slow learner. Her worries about him affect her schoolwork and her peer relationships. They learn that the boy has ADD--"Attention Deficit Disorder"--which is treatable through structuring his behavior and taking medication.

Lowry, Lois. Summer to Die. Laurel Leaf, 1984. (Grades 7-12)
- Thirteen-year-old Meg envies her sister's beauty and popularity. Her feelings don't make it any easier for her to cope with Molly's strange illness and eventual death from leukemia

Lubar, David. Sleeping Freshmen Never Lie. Dutton Juvenile, 2005. (Grades 8-10)
- A humorous account of an awkward freshman boy who's going after the girl. To top it off, his mom is pregnant.

Naylor, Phyllis Reynolds. <u>All Because I'm Older</u>. Dell, 1989. (Grades 6-8)
~ John, who finds being the oldest child very difficult, keeps his sister out of mischief and his brother out of his hair on a trip to the supermart.

Paterson, Katherine. <u>Jacob Have I Loved</u>. Crowell, 1980. (Grades 4-8)
~ Feeling deprived all her life of schooling, friends, mother, and even her name by her twin sister, Louise begins to find her own identity.

Pershall, Mary. <u>You Take the High Road</u>. Penguin, 1990. (Grades 7-12)
~ Samantha's mother has a baby, Nicholas, whose birth creates some unrest in analready uncomfortable family situation, and whose death by drowning at age two causes the family to fall apart.

Rosenberg, Marsha Sarah. <u>Everything You Need to Know when a Brother or Sister Is Autistic</u>. The Rosen Publishing Group, Inc., 2000. (Grades 5-9)
~ Discusses what autism it, how it is diagnosed and treated, and ways that siblings of people with autism can find support.

Seidler, Tor and McCarty, Peter. <u>Brothers Below Zero</u>. HarperTrophy, 2003. (Grades 5-8)
~ Tim can't match up to the athletic, building, and academic talents of his YOUNGER brother John Henry. Fortunately, Tim's great aunt helps him discover his own talent in art.

Werlin, Nancy. <u>Are You Alone on Purpose?</u> Houghton Mifflin Company, 1994. (Grades 7-12)
~ Thirteen-year-old Alison Shandling has always been the good child: calming her autistic twin brother, deflecting her mother's rage, and pleasing her aloof father. Harry Roth has always been the cool kid who tests everyone's limits, especially those of his widowed father, the town's rabbi. The two dislike each other at first sight. When an accident confines Harry to a wheelchair, Alison recognizes his frustration and loneliness and initiates a friendship.

Williams, Carolyn Lynch. <u>A Mother to Embarrass Me</u>. Bantam Doubleday Books for Young Readers, 2003. (Grades 4-8)
~ Many young people can empathize with Laura whose embarrassing mother yodels and walks around in clay-covered pajamas. To make matters worse, Laura's mother just announced that she's pregnant.

Zolotow, Charlotte. <u>If It Weren't for You</u>. Harper & Row, 1966. (Grades 3-6)
~ Two brothers list the advantages they would enjoy, if only they were the only child in the family.

Single-Parent Families

Fine, Anne. <u>My War with Goggle-Eyes</u>. Little, Brown, 1989. (Grades 4-8)
    ~ Kitty is not pleased with her mother's boyfriend, especially his views on the anti-nuclear issue, until unexpected events prompt her, after all, to help him find his place in the family.

Hopkins, Lee Bennett. <u>Mama</u>. Simon & Schuster Books for Young Readers, 1992. (Grades 4-6)
    ~ A young boy describes his mother's struggles to feed, clothe, and protect her two sons using whatever resources she can muster, including stealing.

Klein, Norma. <u>Robbie and the Leap Year Blues</u>. Pocket Books, 1983. (Grades 4-8)
    ~ Eleven-year-old Robbie deals with his parents' joint custody and his approaching puberty.

Masters, Mildred. <u>The House on the Hill</u>. Scholastic, 1982. (Grades 4-8)
    ~ Ten-year-old Jenny visits her divorced father over the summer.

MacLachlan, Patricia. <u>Sarah Plain and Tall</u>. HarperCollins, 1985. (Grades 5-8)
    ~ A story about two children, Anna and Caleb, whose lives are changed forever when their widowed papa advertises for a mail-order bride.

Porter, James. <u>Edge of the Rainforest</u>. International Specialized Book Services, 1991.(Grades 9-12)

~ When a narrow-minded neighbor forces them off their small collective farm in northern Australia, sixteen-year-old Karen and her mother are determined to find a way to keep their home.

Stanek, Muriel. I Won't Go Without a Father. Albert Whitman & Co, 1972. (Grades 4-6)

~ Because he has no father, Steve hesitates to go to the school open house to which fathers and mothers are invited.

Social Issues – Search of Conscience

Buckman, Michelle. <u>Maggie Come Lately</u>. NavPublishing Group, 2007. (Grades 7 and up)

    ⁓ At age 4, Maggie witnessed her mother's suicide. Since then, Maggie has been the parent, housekeeper, and the responsible person in the house since her dad has abandoned his responsibilities, including her two younger brothers. At age 16, Maggie has found a new identity as a popular person, and is struggling with who she really is and what her values are. She really comes into her own after a sexual assault.

Cormier, Robert. <u>The Chocolate War</u>. Laurel Leaf, 1986. (Grades 8–12)

    ⁓ Jerry Renault refuses to sell chocolates during his school's fundraiser and creates quite a stir. It's as if the whole school comes apart at the seams. Tosome, Jerry is a hero, but to others, he becomes a scapegoat--a target for their pent-up hatred. Jerry's just trying to stand up for what he believes in.

Griffin, John Howard. <u>Black Like Me</u>. Signet Book, 1996. (Grades 9 and up)

    ⁓ John Howard Griffin writes about his experiences as a white man who transforms himself with the aid of medication and dye in order to experience firsthand the life of a black man living in the Deep South in the 1950's.

Hansbury, Lorraine. <u>A Raisin in the Sun</u>. Vintage, 1994. (Grades 9 and up)

    ⁓ This play is about a hard working family that does the best they can with what they have. It shows that all choices come with

187

consequences. When the mother comes across a large sum of money, everyone wants to use the money for something different. Mama wanted to buy a house, Walter wanted to invest in a liquor store, and Bennie wanted to use the money for her education to become a doctor. After Mama bought the house she gave the money to Walter to decide what to do with it. Walter made a choice that ruined everyone else's dreams. There are many choices that were made in this play that changed everyone's lives.

Hellman, Lillian. The Little Foxes. Dramatists Play Service Inc, 1995. (Grades 7 and up)
~ A play about a family driven to disaster by overwhelming greed and desire.

Miller, Arthur. The Crucible. Penguin Books, 2003. (Grades 9 and up)
~ The Crucible is based on historical people and real events. Violence follows rumors of witchcraft.

Rose, Reginald. Twelve Angry Men. Dramatic Publications, 1983. (Grades 9 and up)
~ This is a book about twelve jurors who have varied opinions on the issues involving a court case. They expected to come to a quick conclusion and it didn't happen. This is a book about sticking to your opinions whether someone else feels you are right are wrong.

Socio-Economic Issues

Arundel, Honor. <u>Family Failing</u>. Hamilton, 1972. (Grades 8-12)
- ~ Johnna deals with a family falling apart due to unemployment.

Flake, Sharon. <u>Begging for Change</u>. Jump At The Sun, 2003. (Grades 9-12)
- ~ Raspberry Hill steals money from a friend out of desperation when her mother is hospitalized. She begins to feel like her father who steals her money for drugs.

Flake, Sharon. <u>Money Hungry</u>. Jump at the Sun, 2003. (Grades 5-8)
- ~ Raspberry, who's very poor and used to live on the streets, works hard to earn money. When her mother finds the stash, she thinks it's stolen and throws it out the window.

Guy, Rosa and Binch, Caroline. <u>Billy the Great</u>. Doubleday, 1992. (Grades 3-6)
- ~ Billy teaches his parents a lesson about socioeconomic prejudices.

Hansbury, Lorraine. <u>A Raisin in the Sun</u>. Vintage, 1994. (Grades 9 and up)
- ~ This play is about a hard working family that does the best they can with what they have. It shows that all choices come with consequences. When the mother comes across a large sum of money, everyone wants to use the money for something different. Mama wanted to buy a house, Walter wanted to invest in a liquor store, and Bennie wanted to use the money for her education to become a doctor. After Mama bought the house she gave the money to Walter to decide what to do with it. Walter made a choice that ruined

everyone else's dreams. There are many choices that were made in this play that changed everyone's lives.

Harrison, Lisi. The Clique. Little, Brown, 2004. (Grades 6-10)
- This book is all about 7th grade girls who have to learn what to wear and what to do to fit in. Claire gets made fun of because she doesn't fit in the rich community she just moved to.

Hellman, Lillian. The Little Foxes. Dramatists Play Service Inc, 1995. (Grades 7 and up)
- A play about a family driven to disaster by overwhelming greed and desire.

Hopkins, Lee Bennett. Mama. Simon & Schuster Books for Young Readers, 1992. (Grades 4-6)
- A young boy describes his mother's struggles to feed, clothe, and protect her two sons using whatever resources she can muster, including stealing.

Hunt, Nan. Like a Pebble in Your Shoe. HarperCollins, 1997. (Grades 5-8)
- Johnno and his family have lived on the farm for generations. However, a drought causes the family to experience poverty.

Klein, Robin. All in the Blue Unclouded Weather. Puffin, 1993. (Grades 9-12)
- Poverty causes the Mellings to struggle with peer relationships.

Klein, Robin. Hating Alison Ashley. Trumpet Club, 1990. (Grades 7-12)
- Erika Yurken thinks she is tops in her "socially disadvantaged school" until upperclass, golden girl Alison Ashley is enrolled. Erika is envious of the style   and class Alison seems to have.

Mathis, Sharon Bell. Sidewalk Story. Puffin Books, 1986. (Grades 4-8)
- A nine year old girl decides to do something about it when her friend's family is evicted from their apartment.

Porter, James. Edge of the Rainforest. International Specialized Book Services, 1991. (Grades 9-12)
- When a narrow-minded neighbor forces them off their small collective farm in northern Australia, sixteen-year-old Karen and her mother are determined to find a way to keep their home.

Spinelli, Jerry. Maniac Magee. Little, Brown, 1999. (Grades 8-12)
- Maniac Magee is about Jeffrey Magee who lives with his aunt and uncle because his parents died. Jeffrey's uncle and aunt always fight, so Jeffrey runs away. This is a story that includes living in poverty, crossing racial boundaries, and growing up.

Steinbeck, John. <u>Cannery Row</u>. Penguin Books, 1993. (Grades 9-12)

- Cannery Row is about stereotypical good-natured bums and warm-hearted prostitutes living on the fringes of Monterey, California. Steinbeck characterizes lowlifes who are poor but happy.

Stewart, Bridgett and White, Franklin. <u>No Matter What</u>. Blue/Black Press, 2002. (Grades 7-12)

- Bridgett Stewart shares her journey through unthinkable poverty and discusses everything from gaining her own self-respect when no one else would respect her because of where she lived to surviving verbal abuse from classmates, living without a father, school pressures, and her decision to use education as a vehicle from poverty while earning a 4.0 grade point average in tough and trying times. Stewart also discusses self-esteem, alcohol and drugs, and many other topics.

Wolff, Virginia Euwer. <u>Make Lemonade</u>. Scholastic Paperbacks, 1994. (Grades 7-12)

- Two friends who are financially not well-off, show determination to succeed. One friend is the teenage mother of two and the other is determined to be the first in the family to go to college. This is a story that shows trials in life don't need to mean the end of dreams.

Speech Issues/stuttering

Brown, Alan. <u>Lost Boys Never Say Die</u>. Random House Children's Books, 1989. (Grades 4-7)
- Lewis sneaks away from a camp meant to help his stuttering problem. Through his adventures (and 8 weeks alone at home), Lewis meets another boy who helps him build his confidence and overcome his speech problems.

Fusco, Kimberly Newton. <u>Tending to Grace</u>. Laurel-Leaf Books, 2005. (Grades 7-12)
- When Cornelia is abandoned by her mother, she has to fend for herself. Because of her profound stutter, she keeps quiet and stays in remedial classes, despite her desire to be in honors English. She eventually finds someone like her to confide in.

Lears, Laurie. <u>Ben Has Something to Say: A Story About Stuttering</u>. Albert Whitman, 2000. (Grades 3-6)
- Ben is too afraid to communicate. In order to help save a dog, he needs to get up the courage to speak to the owner.

Seidler, Tor. <u>The Silent Spillbills</u>. HarperCollins Publishers, 1998. (Grades 3-6)
- Katerina tries hiding her stutter until she has to speak up to save the silent spillbill bird.

Silverman, Ellen Marie. <u>Jason's Secret</u>. Authorhouse, 2001. (Grades 4-8)
- Jason experiences alienation because of his difficulties with speech. With the help of the school's speech therapist, Jason learns to deal effectively with his problems.

Weber, John. <u>Coping for Kids Who Stutter</u>. The Speech Bin, Incorporated, 1993. (Grades 5-12)
  - A guide for kids who stutter.

Success And Achievement

Bachel, Beverly K. <u>What Do You Really Want? How to Set a Goal and Go for It! A   Guide for Teens</u>. Free Spirit Publishing. (Grades 5 and up)
- Learn how to set goals and then achieve them.

Creamer, Robert W. <u>Babe: The Legend Comes to Life</u>. Simon & Schuster, 1992. (Grades 9 and up)
- Chronicles the road to success as well as the challenges of Babe Ruth.

Erlbach, Arlene. <u>Real Kids Taking the Right Risks Plus How You Can, Too!</u> Free Spirit Publishing. (Grades 5-10)
- First-person stories illustrate how young adults took positive risks to benefit themselves and others.

Graham, John. <u>It's Up to Us The Giraffe Heroes Program for Teens</u>. Free Spirit Publishing. (Grades 7 and up)
- Written to encourage meaning, courage, compassion and personal responsibility in the lives of young adults.

Keller, Helen. <u>Teacher: Anne Sullivan Macy</u>. Larlin Corporation, 1985. (Grades 9 and up)
- Annie had a ferocious temper - even with Helen. She was a perfectionist who pushed Helen to do or try to do many very difficult things. Annie also was determined that Helen should be the best at everything she attempted including the best scholar at Radcliffe College. Helen, however, did not seem to suffer from these pressures in a lasting way - maybe due to her naturally accepting

and gentle nature. Another reason that this book is important is that it shows how and what Helen thought about her life and Annie. Helen's writings about her "Teacher" show that she adored, respected, worried about, and loved Annie. She mourned the fact that Annie did not receive more of the credit for Helen's success.

Lewis, Barbara A. What Do You Stand For? A Kid's Guide to Building Character. Free Spirit Press. (Grades 5 and up)
- This book invites kids to explore and practice honesty, kindness, empathy, integrity, tolerance, patience, respect, and more. Scenarios are set up to help children decide what they'd do.

Lipsyte, Robert. The Contender. HarperTrophy, 1987. (Grades 6-9)
- Alfred is a high-school dropout working at a grocery store. His best friend is in a haze of drugs and violence, and now some street punks are harassing him for something he didn't do. Alfred gathers up the courage to visit Donatelli's Gym, the neighborhood's boxing club. He wants to be a champion--on the streets and in his own life.

Plimpton, George. The Paper Lion: Confessions of a Last-String Quarterback. The Lyons Press, 2003. (Grades 7-12)
- George Plimpton examines how to maintain dignity when success on the field isn't exactly feasible.

Wolff, Virginia Euwer. Make Lemonade. Scholastic Paperbacks, 1994. (Grades 7-12)
- Two friends who are financially not well-off, show determination to succeed. One friend is the teenage mother of two and the other is determined to be the first in the family to go to college. This is a story that shows trials in life don't need to mean the end of dreams.

Suicide

Crutcher, Chris. <u>Chinese Handcuffs</u>. Laurel Leaf, 1991. (Grades 9-12)
- When Dillon Hemingway is forced to witness his brother Preston's suicide, his life understandably seems to fall apart. His quest to make it whole again involves Stacy Ryder, Preston's girlfriend, who is left with more than a memory of Dillon's dead brother, and Jennifer Lawless, a star high school basketball player with a secret too monstrous to tell and too enormous to keep.

Frankel, Bernard and Kranz, Rachel. <u>Straight Talk About Teenage Suicide</u>. Facts on File, 1994.(Grades 7 and up)
- This book on teen suicide keeps calm, provides forthright information, and, more than earlier books, concentrates on loss as a precursor to suicidal feelings and acts. Cross-cultural examination is here, too; e.g., in Japan suicide is often felt to be preferable to living in shame. The book also focuses on several teenagers' stories to make specific points.

Guest, Judith. <u>Ordinary People</u>. Penguin Books, 1993. (Grades 9-12)
- Seventeen-year-old Conrad Jarrett returns to his parents' home and tries to build a new life for himself after spending eight months in a mental institution for attempted suicide.

Leder, Jane Mershky. <u>Dead Serious: A Book for Teenagers About Teenage Suicide</u>. Simon & Schuster, 1987. (Grades 7 and up)
- *Dead Serious* is meant to be a book for teenagers who know someone with suicidal symptoms or who are attempting to cope with the suicidal death of a friend or relative. Leder includes myths and

realities about suicide and concrete suggestions for helping a suicidal friend. Pointers on such things as watching for danger signals and what to say to someone who confides in you are also included.

Nelson, Richard E. and Galas, Judith C. <u>The Power to Prevent Suicide A Guide for Teens Helping Teens</u>. Free Spirit Publishing. (Grades 5 and up)
- Includes up-to-date information on who's at risk, spells out the warning signs, encourages teens to reach out to friends in danger, and tells them how to get help.

Steele, William A. <u>Preventing Teenage Suicide</u>. Academic Therapy, 1983. (Grades 7 and up)
- Gives advice on how to help individuals who feel hopeless.

Survival

Avi. The True Confessions of Charlotte Doyle. HarperCollins Publishers, 1992. (Grades 6-10)
- As the only passenger, and the only female, on a transatlantic voyage in 1832, thirteen-year-old Charlotte finds herself caught between a murderous captain and a mutinous crew.

Crane, Stephan. The Red Badge of Courage. Tor Books, 1997. (Grades 7-12)
- Henry Fleming had no idea how horrible war really was. Now, Henry's fighting for his life and he's scared. He must make a decision, perhaps the most difficult decision he will ever make in his life: save himself-run from the enemy and desert his friends-or fight, be brave, and risk his life.

Desetta, Al, M.A. and Wolin, Sybil, Ph.D. The Struggle to Be Strong True Stories by Teens About Overcoming Tough Times. Free Spirit Publishing. (Grades 7 and up)
- In 30 first-person accounts, teens tell how they overcame major life obstacles, including, drug abuse by loved ones, interracial relationships, abandonment, homosexuality, and more.

Forester, C.S. The African Queen. Back Bay Books, 1984. (Grades 9 and up)
- This novel is about an action in WW I between German forces and what might be called British irregulars. Rose Sayer, sister of an English missionary in German Central Africa, seems an unlikely heroine until her brother dies and she takes responsibility for her

own life. With a gin drinking engineer, Allnutt, the indomitable Miss Sayer sets out on the African Queen, a leaky 30-foot river boat, to strike a blow for England and avenge her brother's death.

Lord, Walter. Day of Infamy. Owl Books, 2001. (Grades 9-12)
~ Walter Lord traces the attack at Pearl Harbor: the spies behind it; the Japanese pilots; the crews on the stricken warships; the men at the airfields and the bases; the Japanese pilot who captured an island single-handedly when he could not get back to his carrier; the generals, the sailors, the housewives, and the children who responded to the attack with anger, numbness, and magnificent courage.

Melville, Herman. Moby Dick. Bantam, 1981. (Grades 5-12)
~ When a wandering sailor looking to be hired onto a whaling ship finds himself on the *Pequod,* little does he know the dire fate that awaits him and his crewmates. The ship's captain, Ahab, is slowly going insane. Having lost a leg in an ill-fated harpoon attack against a fearsome white whale many years before, Ahab vows his revenge against *Moby Dick*--a vow that has become Ahab's deadly obsession.

Remarque, Erich Maria. All Quiet on the Western Front. Ballantine, 1995. (Grades 9-12)
~ This book displays the horror and hopelessness of WWI. Germany's Iron Youth, represented by Paul Baumer and his friends, begin the war as teenagers sure of the justice of their cause and the glory that will be theirs.

Teenage Pregnancy

Anderson, Kristen. <u>The Truth about Sex by High School Senior Girls</u>.
Kristen Anderson, 2005. (Grades 9 and up)
～ *The Truth about Sex by High School Senior Girls* was compiled using
quotes, insights, and statistics about sexual experiences from senior
girls. The book is pro-abstinence, based on the statistic that 74%
of the seniors regret sexual experiences they have had, and it takes
the view that sex is a beautiful and sacred rite to be shared in a fully
committed relationship. The book includes sections on older guys,
the first time, oral sex, STDs, pregnancy, sexual abuse and rape.

Bechard, Margaret. <u>Hanging on to Max</u>. Simon Pulse, 2003. (Grades 10
and up)
～ Sam's girlfriend is pregnant and wants to give up the baby, so
it's up to Sam to take custody when his son is born. But it's Sam's
senior year of high school: and he also must face up to the financial
responsibilities of having a baby.

Carey, Joely. <u>Boys and Sex</u>. Barron's Educational Series, 2002. (Grades 8
and up)
～ This book tells every girl what they should know about boys,
and what boys really want from girls. The author advises girls on
how to deal with emerging sexual emotions and how to say no to
unwanted sex. She also explains the physical facts of sex and the use
of contraceptives, and advises on what to do if pregnancy occurs.
Titles in this series are frank guides intended to help teenage girls
deal with the many uncertainties and challenges that are a part of
growing up.

Davis, Deborah. <u>You Look Too Young to Be a Mom: Teen Mothers Speak Out on Love, Learning, and Success</u>. Perigee Books, 2004. (Grades 7-12)
- This is the story of more than 30 young women who didn't give up on their dreams once they found out they were pregnant. They went on to live the lives they'd always wanted. One woman had her baby, finished high school, then college, and is now in law school. One abused woman in Northern Canada managed to escape her abuser, raise her child, and start a career in music.

Elkind, David. <u>All Grown Up and No Place to Go: Teenagers in Crisis</u>. Perseus Books Group, 1997. (Grades 9 and up)
- Elkind makes a case for protecting teens instead of pressuring them. This book addresses long work hours, rising violence, and pregnancies.

Frost, Helen. <u>Keesha's House</u>. Farrar, Straus, and Giroux, 2003. (Grades 9 and up)
- Joe's mother died when he was young. His aunt took him in when he was 12, and he now owns that house. Keesha's dad is a mean drunk so Joe takes her in. Also in the book is a pregnant 16 year old, a young man whose father threw him out because he is gay, a victim of sexual abuse, a child who's been abandoned then ends up in juvie, and a child whose parents are in jail.

Head, Ann. <u>Mr. and Mrs. Bo Jones</u>. Signet, 1968. (Grades 9 and up)
- A non-romanticized, realistic story of teen pregnancy. Ms. Head writes in a way that is compassionate and understanding, yet realistic.

Heckert, Connie K. <u>To Keera with Love: Abortion, Adoption, or Keeping the Baby, the Story of One Teen's Choice</u>. Rowman & Littlefield Publishers, Inc., 1989. (Grades 8 and up)
- Takes the reader through the decision process once a pregnancy is discovered.

Inclan, Jessica Barksdale. <u>Her Daughter's Eyes</u>. New American Library, 2001. (Grades 9 and up)
- Kate Phillips--17 years old, unmarried, and pregnant--and her younger sister Tyler have been abandoned by their parents. Cancer took their beloved mother two years before, and their father has emotionally left them, choosing to spend his time with his new girlfriend. Kate insists that her baby's existence must remain hidden, but inevitably, the sisters' secrets are discovered, involving the police and children's protective services.

Johnson, Angela. <u>The First Part of Last</u>. Simon & Schuster Children's
Publishing, 2003. (Grades 8 and up)
- Bobby is your classic urban teenaged boy -- impulsive, eager,
restless. On his sixteenth birthday his girlfriend, Nia tells him
she's pregnant. Bobby's going to be a father. Suddenly things like
school and house parties and hanging with friends no longer seem
important as they're replaced by visits to Nia's obstetrician and a
social worker who says that the only way for Nia and Bobby to lead
a normal life is to put their baby up for adoption. Johnson looks at
the male side of teen pregnancy as she delves into one young man's
struggle to figure out what "the right thing" is and then to do it.
No matter what the cost.

Lerman, Evelyn. <u>Teen Moms: The Pain and the Promise</u>. Morning Glory,
1997. (Grades 10 and up)
- The text represents two years of interviews with 50 teens who
were either   pregnant or had children. She explores why teens have
sex, young women's experiences with men, and what motherhood
means to these young mothers. Issues about public assistance and
independence and even an exploration of the positive effects of teen
pregnancy are explored. The last chapter is for adults who want to
have a positive impact on the lives of young adults.

McDonald, Janet.   <u>Spellbound</u>.   HarperCollins Publishers, 2001.
(Grades 9-12)
- Raven's life has been derailed. She never expected she'd be a mother
at sixteen like her best friend, Aisha. Is she going to be just another
high school dropout, a project girl with few prospects? Could be -
except Raven has ambition.

Orcutt, Jane. <u>Lullaby</u>. Tyndale House Publishers, 2002. (Grades 9 and up)
- Merrilee wants only the best for the child she cannot keep.
Nora dreams of being a mother to a child of her own. *Lullaby* is
a Christian story of a courageous teenage girl and a woman who
longs for a baby.

Palardy, Debra J. <u>Sweetie Here's the Best Reason on the Planet to Say No
to Your Boyfriend: Even If You've Already Said Yes</u>. Dorrance Pub
Co, 2000. (Grades 8 and up)
- This book is for adolescents who may have felt pressured to engage
in activities in which they were not always comfortable or completely
willing. It addresses the issue of changing morals in schools and
concerns that this may be enough to make even the most straight-

laced young lady feel that sexual activity is okay. Author Debra J. Palardy presents a collection of lines used by hormone-driven teenage boys to get their girlfriends to engage in sex. She follows through and provides useful comeback and advice for girls, considering their boyfriends' pleas. The author provides the objective wisdom sought by teenagers too embarrassed, timid, or afraid to consult those closet to them. Her guide points out the pitfalls of becoming sexually active, including pregnancy, sexually transmitted disease, and loss of self-esteem. She urges teenage girls to seek guidance from women who have had the time to develop an adult perspective and look back on their own experiences.

Ponton, Lynn, MD. The Sex Lives of Teenagers: Revealing the Secret World of Adolescent Boys and Girls. Plume Books, 2001. (Grades 9 and up)
~ With more and more teenagers having sex by the age of sixteen and others feeling pressured to before they're ready, parents and adolescents must find ways to communicate openly and honestly about a subject that has been ignored for too long. Lynn Ponton, M.D., takes a look at what teenagers have to say about their sexual lives. In a safe forum, without fear of judgment or censorship, teens feel free to speak frankly about their feelings, desires, fantasies, and expectations. And parents give voice to the struggle of coming to terms with their children's emerging sexual identities.   Dr. Ponton opens a dialogue that addresses controversial topics such as pregnancy, abortion, masturbation, sexual orientation, Internet dating, and gender roles. Sensitive subjects such as AIDS and drugs are also explored.

Reynolds, Marilyn. Detour for Emmy. Morning Glory Press, 1993. (Grades 7-12)
~ Longing for the affection and understanding that she doesn't get at home, Emmy is propelled into the arms of overachiever, chorus star, and school hero Arturo. Art promises that he will never hurt her, and their sexual relationship goes too far. They normally use birth control, but one night they don't. Emmy is pregnant with no support from Art.

Reynolds, Marilyn. Too Soon for Jeff: True-To-Life Series from Hamilton High. Morning Glory Press, 1994. (Grades 7-12)
~ Jeff Browning has a plan for his future. So when his girlfriend, Christy, happily informs him she's pregnant, though she had told him she was on the pill, Jeff feels betrayed. Christy refuses to consider

abortion or adoption, and Jeff announces that it is her choice, but it is too soon for him to be a father. As Christy's pregnancy progresses, Jeff is forced to confront his disapproval.

Sparks, Beatrice. Annie's Baby: The Diary of Anonymous, a Pregnant Teenager. Avon, 1998.   (Grades 6 and up)

~ When Annie discovers she's pregnant, she's devastated. She has never felt so alone. With no one she can talk to, she pours her heart out to her diary, confiding her feelings of panic, self-doubt, and the desperate hope that some day she can turn her life around. She decides she wants to keep her baby and dreams of loving and caring for this little person. But after the baby is born, it's in her diary that she faces the agonizing question: Can she really raise this child on her own?

Swisher, Karin L., Leone, Bruno, and O'Neil, Terry. Teenage Sexuality: Opposing Viewpoints. Gale Group, 1994. (Grades 9 and up)

~ An examination of birth control, sex education, STDs, homosexuality, pregnancy, and changes in the attitudes toward teenage sexuality and morality. The book explores a wide range of opinions and perspectives. *(Doris A. Fong)*

Wild, Margaret. One Night. Alfred A. Knopf, Inc., 2004. (Grades 9 and up)

~ In this novel written in free verse and narrated by alternating characters, a teenaged girl decides to have her baby and care for it on her own after a "one night stand" results in pregnancy.

Wolff, Virginia Euwer.   Make Lemonade. Scholastic Paperbacks, 1994. (Grades 7-12)

~ Two friends who are financially not well-off, show determination to succeed. One friend is the teenage mother of two and the other is determined to be the first in the family to go to college. This is a story that shows trials in life don't need to mean the end of dreams.

Zimmerman, Martha. Should I Keep My Baby? Bethany House Publishers, 1983. (Grades 8 and up)

~ The author offers straight-to-the-heart advice on getting immediate medical attention, knowing who to tell, evaluating your alternatives, choosing life for your baby rather than aborting, deciding if you're ready for marriage and motherhood, and understanding adoption.

Additional Books & Their Topics Found to Be Helpful

_____

_____

_____

_____

_____

_____

_____

_____

_____

_____

_____

_____

CPSIA information can be obtained at www.ICGtesting.com
Printed in the USA
LVOW061809130312

272905LV00007B/5/P